Punctuation
Made Easy in O

The **One Hour Wordpower** *series*

WORD BANK: Expanding Your Vocabulary
WORD CHECK: Using Words Correctly
GOOD GRAMMAR IN ONE HOUR
THE NAME BOOK
THE SECRETS OF SPEED READING
GUIDE TO WORDPLAY AND WORD GAMES
CRISP CLEAR WRITING IN ONE HOUR
SPELL CHECK: 1000 Most Misspelled Words
SAY IT RIGHT: 1000 Most Mispronounced Words
PUNCTUATION MADE EASY IN ONE HOUR
WORD CHECK 2: Over 1000 Nasty New Problem Words
WORLD WORD BANK: A Guide to Foreign Words and
  Sayings
Dictionary of ABBREVIATIONS AND ACRONYMS
The One Hour Wordpower DICTIONARY

One Hour Wordpower

Punctuation
*Made Easy
in One Hour*

GRAHAM KING

Mandarin
in association with
The Sunday Times

A Mandarin Paperback
PUNCTUATION MADE EASY IN ONE HOUR

First published in Great Britain 1994
by Mandarin Paperbacks
an imprint of Reed Consumer Books Ltd
Michelin House, 81 Fulham Road, London SW3 6RB
and Auckland, Melbourne, Singapore and Toronto

Copyright © Graham King 1994
The right of Graham King to be identified as the Author
of these works has been asserted in accordance
with the Copyrights, Designs and Patents Act 1988

A CIP catalogue record for this title
is available from the British Library
ISBN 0 7493 1878 3

Printed and bound in Great Britain
by Cox & Wyman Ltd, Reading, Berkshire

Contents

The definitive sources for word meanings and usage in *Punctuation Made Easy in One Hour* were derived from *The Oxford English Dictionary*, *Collins Complete Dictionary* and the *Chambers Dictionary*.

Consultant on grammar and linguistics: Paul Coggle, Senior Lecturer in German, University of Kent in Canterbury.

Acknowledgements

The following works have been consulted during the writing of *Punctuation Made Easy in One Hour* and thanks are due to their authors and publishers:

Bryson, Bill. *Mother Tongue*. Penguin, 1990.

Fowler, H. W. *A Dictionary of Modern English Usage*. OUP, 1991.

Gowers, Sir Ernest. *The Complete Plain Words*. HMSO, 1986.

Greenbaum, Sidney. *An Introduction to English Grammar*. Longman, 1991.

Greenbaum, S. and Whitcut, J. *Guide to English Usage*. Longman, 1991.

Howard, Philip. *The State of the Language*. Penguin, 1986.

Laird, Charlton. *The Word*. Simon & Schuster, 1981.

Murray-Smith, Stephen. *Right Words: A Guide to English Usage in Australia*. Penguin, 1990.

Partridge, Eric. *You Have a Point There*. Routledge, 1983.

Partridge, Eric. *Usage and Abusage*. Penguin, 1963.

Partridge, Eric. *What's the Good Word?* Times Books NY, 1982.

Safire, William. *On Language*. Times Books NY, 1981.

Sunday Times, The. *Style and Usage Guide*. 1993.

Times, The. *English Style and Usage Guide*. Times Books, 1992.

Todd, L. and Hancock, I. *International English Usage*. Routledge, 1990.

Waldhorn, A. and Zeiger, A. *English Made Simple*. Butterworth-Heinemann, 1991.

'The writer who has to torment his mind
about the punctuation of a passage
does well to enquire whether he is
not struggling with something he should
not have written, or should have
written differently.'

Jacques Bazun

Introduction

In its widest sense, punctuation is the clear presentation of the written language.

Or, as one newspaper advises its writers, punctuation is '*a courtesy designed to help readers to understand a story without stumbling.*' It is a convenience rather than an integral part of the language; it is nuts and bolts rather than girders.

There is a strong view that punctuation is more important than spelling. Dr Temple, a former Archbishop of York, thought so. 'Now spelling is one of the decencies of life, like the proper use of knives and forks,' he wrote in 1938. But, 'if you are getting your commas, semicolons and full stops wrong, it means that you are not getting your thoughts right, and your mind is muddled.'

Despite the importance of punctuation in effective communication, there seems today to be a woeful indifference to and ignorance about using even its simplest forms. Unfortunately the whole business has got itself a bad name – or, rather, bad names: boring, contradictory, unnecessary, impenetrable, tedious, terrifying. None of these is deserved, and this book sets out not only to prove it but to take the perils out of punctuation simply, efficiently and entertainingly.

You're looking at a system that is some 2,500 years old. The Greeks came up with the germ of the idea but it took until the tenth century for our present system to emerge and another 700 years for it to acquire its final polish. It became very elaborate. Its more skilled practitioners – say, Jane Austen and Charles Dickens – loved to punctuate, and their stately prose and long, rambling sentences are speckled with all manner of punctuation marks.

Today, though, we're speeding along. Homogenisation is the name of the game. Why bother about the difference between a comma and a semicolon, or a colon and a dash? Why bother anyway when a dash will punctuate just about everything? The pressure to abandon all but the simplest points of punctuation is greater than ever now that increasing numbers are learning basic English as their second language; the niceties of the apostrophe are understandably lost on a student grappling with the cross-grained contradictions of simplified English.

Fortunately there is also a growing number of discriminating users of English who wish to master the craft and art of punctuation and to use it with flair and even enjoyment. It is to this group that *Punctuation Made Easy in One Hour* is directed.

Is there a trick secret in understanding punctuation?

No, but it does help if you know something about its past. Two hundred years ago most punctuation took its cues from speech. This was a period when the predominant practice of reading aloud, with its pauses and dramatic stresses, was translated into written punctuation – rhetorical punctuation.

A hundred years on, with increased literacy, the spoken word gave way to the written. The stress now was on meaning rather than dramatic effect, and rhetorical (or oratorical) punctuation bowed to a more logical system.

Today we think we have a practical blend of both: a system capable of conveying force, intonation, urgency, tension, rhythm and passion while never abandoning its duty to consistency and clarity of meaning.

Here's an example of how a sentence might have been written, say, 150 years ago, compared with the same sentence today. The first reflects the pauses of speech: it is meant to be *heard* rather than read. The second is directed primarily to the eye and the mind, rather than to the ear:

Everyone in the cast knew, that Pamela would wish to be the star performer, and once having achieved that status would look down on the rest.

Everyone in the cast knew that Pamela would wish to be the star performer and, once having achieved that status, would look down on the rest.

A system of punctuation was inevitable with the invention and growth of printing, and publishers have played a vital part in its development. With punctuation, books became easier to read and more attractive, and the self-interested publishers made certain the system was refined and permanent. Even today punctuation correctness is almost an obsession with the publishing industry.

But if this gives you the impression that punctuation consists of a strict set of rigid rules, it is wrong. What rules exist have been assembled over some 400 years without agreement ever being reached on the full set. Some rules are, of course, obligatory, like finishing a sentence with a full stop and not a comma. But others are optional, subject to context, style and, increasingly, common sense. Skilful writers have long played at breaking the rules, creatively deploying punctuation to achieve fresh stylistic effects.

The grammatical climate now is one of relaxation. Sentences are noticeably shorter, heavily influenced by the column-controlled brevity of newspapers and magazines. The need for the complicated division of long sentences has disappeared. Commas are dropped where the meaning remains unaffected. Stops after abbreviations are disappearing in a general quest for typographic unfussiness. The majority of the English-using population probably goes through life without ever using, on paper, any punctuation marks other than the comma, dash and full stop.

Simplicity, however, does not equate with sloppiness. Most of us know that it is pointless to write an unintelligible sentence; and that what we write will not be read unless it clearly conveys its intended meaning.

Fewer among us realise that, while what we write might be clear enough, it will, to quote Edgar Allan Poe, be 'deprived of half its force – its spirit – its point – by improper punctuation.'

A Victorian Schoolmistress's Rules of Punctuation

Sentences start with a *Capital letter*,
So as to make your writing better.
Use a *full stop* to mark the end.
It closes every sentence penned.
The *comma* is for short pauses and breaks,
And also for lists the writer makes.
Dashes – like these – are for thoughts
   by the way.
They give extra information (so do
   brackets, we may say).
These two dots are *colons*: they pause
   to compare.
They also do this: list, explain and prepare.
The *semicolon* makes a break; followed by a clause.
It does the job of words that link; it's also
   a short pause.
An *apostrophe* shows the owner of anyone's things,
And it's also useful for shortenings.
I'm so glad! He's so mad! We're having such
   a lark!
To show strong feelings use an *exclamation mark*!
A *question mark* follows What? When? Where? Why?
   and How?
Do you? Can I? Shall We? Give us your answer now!
"*Quotation marks*" enclose what is said,
Which is why they're sometimes called "*speech
   marks*" instead.

Units of Space

Sentences and Paragraphs

Space is a basic form of punctuation. It separates words, sentences, paragraphs and larger units such as chapters. Historically, in medieval manuscripts and early books, sentences were separated by a variety of decorative devices. But with the advent of printing this labour-intensive practice was dropped in favour of plain spaces: small spaces between words, larger spaces between sentences, and fresh lines – often indented – for paragraphs, as in this book.

Early capital letters were typically highly ornamented to draw attention to the start of a sentence. Today, although we have dropped the ornamentation, the capital still conventionally serves as a marker for the beginning of sentences, proper names and is also used for a number of other functions.

The sentence is about the most common of all grammatical units. We speak in sentences. The most untutored letter-writers among us will use them while ignoring every other form of punctuation. So the sentence seems a good place to begin a discussion about this apparently boring but – and I hope you will agree well before reading half-way through this book – in reality wonderfully fascinating subject.

So, what is a sentence? The *Oxford English Dictionary*'s famous definition is: '*Such portion of a composition or utterance as extends from one full stop to another.*' And there are dozens more stabs by eminent grammarians at defining what a sentence is and is not, which is surprising because the unit has been around for some 1,500 years. The functions of sentences are, however, straightforward:

- To make statements
- To ask questions
- To request action
- To express emotion

It's also reasonable to say that a sentence should express a single idea, and that it should be complete in thought and complete in construction. Like this:

> The rare great crested newt was once called the great warty newt.

The sentence can be quite elastic, and punctuation allows us to expand this useful unit:

> The rare great crested newt, which is native to Britain and rarely exceeds fifteen centimetres in length, was once called the great warty newt.

You'll notice how the cunning commas have allowed us to double the length of the sentence without losing any of its original clarity.

Sentences can also shrink, often alarmingly:

> *'Don't!'*

That single word, providing it is given meaning by other words or thoughts surrounding it, is a true sentence, or, more correctly, a sentence fragment:

> I went over to the door and tried to open it.
> *'Don't!'*
> I spun around, searching for the owner of the angry voice. In the darkness, a face appeared, ...

You can see here that not only the surrounding words, but also a range of spaces and punctuation marks, help to give that single word the meaning intended.

A question that crops up with worrying regularity is, '*How long should a sentence be?*' The pat answer is, neither too long nor too short. A sensible approach is to regard short sentences as more easily digestible; on the other hand an endless succession of staccato sentences can be irritating to the reader. It really comes back to judgement. Good writers will read their work, aloud or 'mentally aloud', as they proceed; that way the sentences will form themselves into a logical, interesting, economical and, with luck, elegant flow of thought.

Here is a piece of prose that is more torture than sentence:

A person shall be treated as suffering from physical disablement such that he is either unable to walk or virtually unable to do so if he is not unable or virtually unable to walk with a prosthesis or an artificial aid which he habitually wears or uses or if he would not be unable or virtually unable to walk if he habitually wore or used a prosthesis or an artificial aid which is suitable in his case.

No doubt that was written by somebody with the expectation that it would be understood, but it defies understanding. Yet what it tries to say is something very simple, and which can be unambiguously expressed in our ideal sentence, '*complete in thought and complete in construction*':

Persons are regarded as physically disabled if they always need an artificial aid to walk.

The Paragraph

The most quoted definition of a paragraph is that of Sir Ernest Gowers, who wrote in *The Complete Plain Words* that it is 'a unit of thought, not of length . . . homogeneous in subject matter and sequential in treatment of it.' *The Times*, in advising its journalists, adds: 'Rarely should a paragraph in *The Times* be of only one sentence, least of all a short one, unless special emphasis is needed. Long paragraphs are tedious but short ones are jerky and can be equally hard to follow. The best advice is to remember Gowers and ask, before pressing the paragraph key, "Have I finished that thought?".'

All very well, but of all the units of punctuation the paragraph is the least precise and the most resistant to rules. Sometimes they are indented, sometimes not. Quite often, the first paragraph under a heading is not indented, although all subsequent paragraphs are. Browse through a handful of books and you will see that paragraphs can consist of a single line or a single word or leviathan examples which ramble on for a page or more.

Here are some useful pointers. Think of the end of a paragraph as a sort of breathing space for both speaker and listener. The speaker has reached a point of fresh departure, and the listener needs a break from concentration. In writing, a new paragraph marks a break or change in the flow of thought, which is as good a reason as any to begin on a fresh line.

Capital Letters

Capital letters are a form of punctuation in that they help to guide the eye and mind through a text. Try this:

mi5 is the branch of the british intelligence organisation responsible for internal security and counter-espionage in britain. mi6 is the branch responsible for international espionage. the us has its fbi and the republic of ireland its g2. spies love abbreviations! then, in britain, there is mi1, directorate of military intelligence, and mi8, the radio security service, besides mi11 and mi9. not surprisingly, each of these clandestine outfits spawns even more shadowy initials. di, sf, gc&cs and, ultimately, wx, the butlins of the spy world.

That is a paragraph shorn of capital letters. It's readable, with some effort, but how much easier would the eye glide through it were it guide-posted with capitals at the start of each sentence – not to mention capitalised abbreviations!

The use of capital letters to indicate the beginning of sentences and for many abbreviations is clear enough, but a good deal of mystery surrounds the use of capitals in other areas of writing. Here, then, is a brief guide to capitals:

Sentences	Open every sentence with a capital letter.
First Person Pronoun	I said I was going out.
Certain Exclamations	Oh Ahrrgh! Ooh Whoa! Wow!
Personification	The family gods were Hope and Charity; Faith was abandoned years ago.
Proper Names	These include the names of people (John, Margaret Thatcher); places (Mt Everest, London, Asia); titles (*From Here to Eternity, Sunset Boulevard, Ode on a Grecian Urn, A Day In The Life*); epithets (Iron Duke, Iron

Lady, Birmingham Six);
nicknames (Tubby Isaacs,
Leadfoot Evans); races of
people (Aztecs, Prussians,
Shawnees, Eskimos).

Trade Names,
Trade Marks
Hoover, Meccano, Peugeot,
Xerox, Coca Cola, Kentucky
Fried Chicken, Cellophane.

The Deity
God, Father, Almighty, Holy
Ghost, Holy Spirit, Jesus Christ,
Allah, Buddha. Also: Bible, New
Testament, Koran, Talmud, etc.
Religions are also capitalised:
Judaism, Christianity, Catholic,
Protestant, Buddhist, Baptists,
Presbyterians.

The Calendar
Monday, March, Good Friday,
St Patrick's Day.

History
Cambrian Era, Carboniferous,
Middle Ages, Georgian,
Victorian, Edwardian.

Our Rulers
Chancellor of the Exchequer,
Secretary of State, House of
Commons, British Parliament,
Government House, Her
Majesty's Government,
Conservative party and Labour
party (note the small 'p').

Royalty
The Queen, Duke of Edinburgh,
Prince of Wales, Princess of
Wales, Duke and Duchess of
York, Queen Elizabeth the
Queen Mother, Princess Royal
(Princess Anne).

Heavenly Bodies
Earth, Venus, Mars, Uranus,
Ursa Major, Great Bear, Halley's
Comet.

Geographical	The West, the East, the Orient, Northern Hemisphere, New World, British Commonwealth.
Flora and Fauna	Arab horse, Shetland pony, bulldog. With scientific names, the first name, the genus, is capitalised: *Agaricus bisporus* is the commercial mushroom. Such names are usually italicised.
Titles	Sir Thomas More, Lord Asquith, Mrs Brown.
Satirised References	In Crowd, Bright Young Things, Non-U, Heavy Brigade, She Who Must Be Obeyed.

As a rule, generalities are spelt entirely lower-case, while specifics usually require capitals. This can sometimes cause confusion:

- George Bush, a former president, met President Clinton.
- 'Actually, I *am* Prince Charles,' declared the prince.
- The North is traditionally north of the Wash.
- Fleet Street is a short street with a long history.
- Did the Venetians really invent the venetian blind?

Despite all that advice, the capital letter is sometimes required – or not required – where we least expect it. Here are a few examples of cryptic capitals.

army	lower-case, but *British Army*, *Italian Army*
dog breeds	lower-case: *rottweiler*, *lurcher*, *bulldog*, but *Labrador*, *Scotch terrier*, *Afghan hound* etc.
embassy	lower-case, as in *Nicaraguan embassy*

government	lower-case, as in *British government*, but *Her Majesty's Government*
Hague, The	both words capitalised
Jacuzzi	a trade name, so capitalised
Liberal Democrat	capitalised, but *Liberal Democratic party*
local government	council, but *Kent County Council, Bath City Council, Enfield Borough Council* etc. *Lord Mayor of London*, but when not used as the full title, use *mayor*, as in: The *mayor* made a fine speech
member of Parliament	lower-case, except when abbreviated: *MP*
national anthem	lower-case
National Health Service	and *NHS*
navy, naval	but *Royal Navy, Chinese Navy*. Ranks are capitalised: *Admiral, Captain, Petty Officer*, etc.
nazi	lower-case when derisive; *Nazi* when referring to the former German political party
New Year's Day	but *happy new year*
Old Master	when referring to *Old Master* paintings
pope	but *Pope Paul, Pope John*, etc.
post office branch	and *post office services*, but *the Post Office*
Pre-Raphaelite	not *pre-Raphaelite painting*
Reverend	Such titles are capitalised, but the *Rev Adam Black* is preferred. Also *Fr O'Brien, Sister Brown, Mother Teresa*, the *Right Rev Thomas Jones*. Official church names and titles are a mass of contradictions (no pun intended): *holy orders* but *Holy*

	Communion; Mass but *requiem Mass; primate* but *the Primate of All England* (*the Archbishop of Canterbury*)
right wing	always lower-case: *the right, the left, leftwing, rightwinger*
Romany	the 'correct' definition of the true gypsy, and emphatically not a 'new age traveller'
Scottish nationalist	but *Scottish National Party*
Scouts	*Guides* and *Cub Scouts* are all capitalised
Seasons	*spring, summer, autumn, winter*
Spiritualism	and *Spiritualists* are capitalised
Test match	as with *Lord's*, is always capitalised
Tote, the	is capitalised, but *totalisator* isn't
Underground	*London Underground* and the *Tube* are capitalised
Van	when writing Dutch names observe the convention that *van* is in lower-case when part of the full name (Hans *van* Meegeren, Vincent *van* Gogh, Anthony *van* Dyke) but capitalised when used only with the surname (*Van* Meegeren, *Van* Gogh, *Van* Dyke)
von	In Germanic names, always in lower-case
World War	capitalise, as in *World War I, World War II*. The use of *first world war* or *second world war* is now generally preferred

Devices for Separating and Joining

The Full Stop

Now we shrink from the paragraph to a minuscule dot: the full stop, full point or period. Minuscule it may be but, like atoms and germs, it packs a potent power. The full stop is the most emphatic, abrupt and unambiguous of all the punctuation marks.

The stop is also probably the most used mark, partly because we need it so much, and partly because virtually everyone knows how to use it. A good guess would be that half the population gets by with just two punctuation marks – the full stop and the occasional dash.

Here's a typical fictional passage displaying a variety of punctuation marks; the full stop, though, is easily the most predominant.

> With intense frustration, Giles grabbed the man, surprising him. 'No you don't!' he shouted.
>
> The man recovered, fighting back. Fiercely. Savagely.
>
> Hard breathing. The wincing thud of fists. An alarming stream of blood from Giles's eye.
>
> Pulses racing, they glared at one another, each daring the other to make the next move.

That's stylised prose, and could be criticised for its over-use of sentence fragments rather than complete sentences. But here the heavy-handed application of the full stop is deliberate, for we can see what the writer is getting at – the punch, punch, punch effect of a fist-fight.

We can also see from the above example just how essential the full stop is, although there have been numerous attempts to do without it. One of the most famous examples is the Penelope chapter in James Joyce's *Ulysses*:

'. . . a quarter after what an earthly hour I suppose they're just getting up in China now combing out their pigtails for the day well soon have the nuns ringing the angelus theyve nobody coming in to spoil their sleep except an odd priest or two for his night office the alarm clock next door . . .

[*until about 1,000 words later*]

'. . . and first I put my arms around him yes and drew him down to me so he could feel my breasts all perfume yes and his heart was going like mad and yes I said yes I will Yes.'

But you did notice the full stop at the very end, didn't you? At least Joyce had to observe the rule that every sentence, however long, must end with a full stop or a variation of it.

Of course that's an extreme case, with Joyce chucking out all stops to achieve the effect of a stream of conscious outpouring. At the other end of the scale is prose that, well, goes full-stop-mad, such as this excerpt from Alain Arias-Misson's *Confessions* (1974). The style was considered innovative in the early 1970s:

'Fischer shot a glance at me. Listen Fischer, I said, is there any way out of here? You are not an initiate, he said. Of course I addressed myself to him because I hoped there might be a model in his game. I watched the pieces under his eyes.

Ah yes, I said, I see. How curious, I thought, as I stood up, that I hadn't realised it until now. I didn't know what move to make next. The next move may be death, he said. I moved my piece and walked out of the room. He was no longer outside of the game. He was of course a free agent. I knew it would be necessary to listen carefully, in this suspended atmosphere. The master player had shown me a trick or two. It was a matter of life and death.'

Again, the author is using punctuation for a special effect, in this case to convey something of the heart-arresting tension of an important chess game.

From these examples you can understand why it is difficult to lay down rules for punctuation. Both examples are, by literary standards, correct, compelling and readable, but in the hands of lesser writers the extremes of under-use and over-use are best avoided.

More important in good writing is when and where to use the full stop. Some writers might be tempted to link the following two thoughts to make a single sentence:

The sofa served them well for thirty years, and the best store for sofas is owned by the Mowgli Brothers.

Now, although the two thoughts are related by a common subject – sofas – they really make two quite separate points. The crudest way to deal with this situation is to express the thoughts by separating them with a full stop, thus forming two sentences:

The sofa served them well for thirty years. The best store for sofas is owned by the Mowgli Brothers.

But this solution feels uncomfortable, doesn't it? Although it is more logical and grammatically correct, we are still left to ponder over the relationship between the Mowgli Brothers' sofa store and the serviceable thirty-year-old sofa. Was it purchased from the Mowgli Brothers? If so, why not use this fact to connect the two thoughts:

> The sofa served them well for thirty years. It was supplied by the Mowgli Brothers, who own the best store for sofas.

Or, dispensing with the full stop:

> The sofa which had served them well for thirty years came from the Mowgli Brothers, the best store for sofas.

But what if the sofa was purchased elsewhere? If this were the case, the presentation of the facts requires a different construction entirely. Perhaps something like this:

> Although the Mowgli Brothers' store supplies the finest sofas, their own sofa had served them well for thirty years.

Or, alternatively, the thoughts could be separated with a full stop:

> The Mowgli Brothers' store is famous for its sofas. Their own sofa, however, had served them well for thirty years.

Finally, here are some words of wisdom about full stops and using them to form sentences:

- Keep sentences variable in length, but generally short.

- Using long sentences doesn't necessarily make you a good writer.
- To use *only* full stops is as unnatural as walking without using your knee-joints.

Full Stops and Abbreviations

Full stops have been traditionally used to make many abbreviations, or contractions. The old convention was to use stops for chopped-off words:

doz. Sat. Oct. Prof. Staffs.

but not for abbreviations formed by the first and last letters of a word:

Mr   Dr   Pd (paid)   gdn (garden)   mfr (manufacturer).

Thus, by the rules, *per cent.* was considered a contraction in the first category because it abbreviated *per centum*!

All this, however, has gone by the board because, increasingly and remorselessly, the stops are being abandoned in favour of speed, economy and cleaner typography. You will, of course, still see plenty of full stops in abbreviations, but here is a sample of the new order:

Formerly	**Now** (mostly)
6 a.m.	6 am
Dr. Jones	Dr Jones
e.g.	eg
1472 A.D.	1472 AD
Jan. 16	Jan 16
Wm. Shakespeare	Wm Shakespeare
viz.	viz
R.S.V.P.	RSVP
Capt. Johns, D.F.C.	Capt Johns, DFC
U.K.	UK

The Comma

The comma is the most flexible, most versatile of all the punctuation marks. Because it is the least emphatic mark it is also the most complex and subtle. Not surprisingly, therefore, many people confess to feeling a nagging uncertainty about using commas.

While the full stop brings proceedings to a grinding halt, the comma, with its ability to build complex sentences, enlarges upon thoughts, joins them to further thoughts and afterthoughts, and plays with them. A writer with full command of the comma can have a ball. Here's the English humorist Alan Coren displaying an enviable skill with this little beast in a passage in which the commas are like the carefully placed hoofprints of a horse lining up for a jump, and then – a long, soaring comma-less passage follows before the full stop landing!

'Until I was 40, I was utterly urban, uneasy in any surroundings more arborious than a sparsely tubbed patio, and knowing no more of wildlife than that a starling was probably taller than a stoat. As for the horse, I regarded it primarily as something to watch out for in French casseroles. But 40 is a critical age, a time for last-ditch stands, so I bought that last ditch in the New Forest, and the hovel that leaned over it, and enough land for the kids to run about and get tetanus in, somewhere, in short, which would allow me to escape into that sweet Arcadia where deer eat the rockery and mice eat the roof and ponies eat the hedges and a man can be snug in his nocturnal cot and hear naught save the soporific sound of death-watch beetles laughing at the inadequacy of creosote.'

Now that, to a comma freak, is about as good as you'll find anywhere in the language. Note, too, that Coren even gets away with a comma (after '*get tetanus in, . . .*') where ordinary grammatically-correct mortals would have placed a semicolon.

But back to earth. Perhaps the most resilient myth about commas is that they indicate breath pauses. There was some truth in this when the language was more orally inclined, but today commas have all but succumbed to grammatical logic.

> Every year over the British Isles, half a million meteorites enter the atmosphere.

You can hear the lecturer intoning this, can't you – with a dramatic pause before announcing '*half a million*'. Try it. But when you write it as a sentence you find that the comma is quite redundant:

> Every year over the British Isles half a million meteorites enter the atmosphere.

Most writing today demands that commas be logical, but if you are a novelist, reporting a character's speech, you would be correct to use what are called 'rhetorical commas' when the character takes a natural breath.

Contemporary writing is far less rambling and rhetorical than it was in Dickens' day. Here's a not untypical sentence from *Martin Chuzzlewit*:

> 'Then there was George Chuzzlewit, a gay bachelor cousin, who claimed to be young, but had been younger, and was inclined to corpulency, and rather overfed himself – to the extent, indeed, that his eyes were strained in their sockets, as if with constant surprise; and he had such an obvious disposition to pimples, that the bright spots on his cravat, the rich pattern on his

waistcoat, and even his glittering trinkets, seemed to have broken out upon him, and not to have come into existence comfortably.'

After reaching for the indigestion tablets you can tot up the commas: twelve in all, plus a dash and a semicolon. If you were disposed to write such a sentence today, you would probably use only five commas, six at most. Try it.

But the over-use of commas still survives in sentences wrought by writers, possibly Librans, who can't make their minds up. Their sentences tend to be hedged with *ifs*, *buts*, *maybes* and pontifications:

It is, curiously, surprising when, say, you hear your name announced in a foreign language, or even in a strange accent.

Here's another sample, which can be rewritten without any commas at all:

He had not, previously, met the plaintiff, except when, in 1954, he had, unexpectedly, found himself in Paris.

Before we get too glib about comma removal, here is a well-comma'd sentence written by a craftsman, detective story writer Julian Symons. In this case you will find it rather difficult to remove any of the commas without causing confusion or disturbing the flow:

'Waugh had already perfected his technique in writing dialogue, by which fragmented, interjectory, often apparently irrelevant, but, in fact, casually meaningful conversations carry along much of the plot, avoiding the need for description.'

32

Let's look a little closer at comma reduction by taking a simple sentence:

A My hobby, train-spotting, is, to many, a joke.
B My hobby, train-spotting, is to many, a joke.
C My hobby, train-spotting, is to many a joke.
D My hobby train-spotting is to many, a joke.
E My hobby train-spotting is to many a joke.

Pedants might claim that all these sentences differ in shades of meaning, but, really, to the average reader they all mean the same thing; so we are left with choosing which one we would use to get our point across simply, economically, unambiguously and fluently. Which would you choose? My own choice would be **C**, but it is a personal one and not one I would impose on others.

The ability to recognise where commas are needed and where they are not may be an acquired skill but it is worth pursuing. Merely scanning a sentence will usually tell you. The writer of the following sentence was either afraid of commas or intent on speed of delivery:

The land is I believe owned by the City Council.

I think most of us would call for commas here after *is* and *believe*, and the grammatical reason for this is discussed later in this chapter. A more serious lapse occurs when the lack of commas leads to ambiguity, and even hilarity:

As the car slowly sank over the road the neighbours laughed uproariously.

Only a comma after *sank* will rescue the meaning from this sentence. A better idea, however, would be to rewrite:

As the car slowly sank, the neighbours over the road laughed uproariously.

As a general rule, where dropping a comma doesn't endanger understanding but instead helps the flow of a sentence, leave it out.

No, Thanks!

How often do we write, or see written, 'No thanks' – or, more commonly, say it – without separating or mentally separating the two words with a comma? It's a phrase that seems to have lost all its meaning, which is, 'No, thanks', i.e. *No (I decline), thanks (but thank you all the same)*. Using the two words without the separating comma amounts to a rude rejection: 'Would I want one of your cakes? No thanks!'

Here are three examples of sentences containing commas which shouldn't be there:

The trophy presented to the winner, was the one donated by the local butcher.

They left him, bleeding on the roadside.

You can never foretell, what the weather will be like.

Just as common an error is the 'comma splice': the use of a comma in place of a linking word to unite two sentences in the mistaken belief that it will form a single sentence:

The house is large, it has five bedrooms.

This is not what we regard as a grammatical sentence, but there are several ways to make it one:

The house is large; it has five bedrooms.
The house is large because it has five bedrooms.
The house is large and has five bedrooms.
The house is large, with five bedrooms.

Simple? You would think so, but hitching a second sentence to another with a mere comma is not confined to the inexperienced writer. Here's the novelist E. M. Forster in *A Passage to India*:

'Chance brought her into his mind while it was in this heated state, he did not select her, she happened to occur among the throng of soliciting images, a tiny splinter, and he impelled her by his spiritual force to that place where completeness can be found.'

One hesitates to correct a master, but surely a full stop is called for after '*heated state*', and either a colon or semicolon after '*select her*'. But you really begin to wonder when you find the great stylist W. Somerset Maugham scattering comma splices throughout the pages of his *Of Human Bondage*:

'. . . often he sat and looked at the branches of a tree silhouetted against the sky, it was like a Japanese print . . .'
'You must congratulate me, I got my signatures yesterday . . .'
'I looked in on my way out, I wanted to tell you my news . . .'

In all three cases remedial action is called for, with the commas being replaced with full stops, or at the very least, with semicolons. In the last two sentences a linking word like *because* could happily substitute for the commas.

Despite their faulty construction, at least the meaning of the offending sentences is clear. That, however, can't be said of the following group of miscreants where commas, or lack of them, create ambiguity:

They were sick and tired of the seemingly endless journey.
They were sick, and tired of the seemingly endless journey.

Brenda and Ian didn't fall in love because they liked their privacy too much.
Brenda and Ian didn't fall in love, because they liked their privacy too much.

At the Coronation, he heard, many of the guests had to stand for six hours.
At the Coronation he heard many of the guests had to stand for six hours.

My son Frederick Fortescue invented the whoopee cushion.
My son, Frederick Fortescue, invented the whoopee cushion.

All four examples here are slightly subtler versions of the following old chestnuts:

The animal spun an arrow through its heart.
The animal spun, an arrow through its heart.

Common sense suggests that, to make sense, a comma is necessary after *spun*.

This second chestnut illustrates how the position of a comma can alter meaning:

To be honest, cashiers don't go home late.
To be honest cashiers, don't go home late.

But to return to the four main sets of examples. In the first, the simple addition of a comma after *sick* alters the meaning of the sentence dramatically; without the comma they are merely 'fed up', but with the comma they are rather more worse for wear.

In the case of Brenda and Ian, the first sentence could imply that Brenda and Ian *did* fall in love, but not for the reason that they liked their privacy. With a comma after *love*, however, it is clear that their budding relationship failed because they were protective of their privacy.

At the Coronation, the two commas are vital to understanding the sentence. With the commas, it seems that he wasn't actually present at the event but had heard somewhere that people had to stand for six hours. Without the commas we are led to believe – although it is not absolutely clear – that he *was* at the Coronation, where he heard about the plight of some of the guests. Both sentences are somewhat ambiguous and would benefit from reconstruction. There is no doubt about the meaning of this version:

While attending the Coronation he heard that many of the guests had to stand for six hours.

The final example illustrates a trap most of us fall into from time to time. While both sentences tend to look as though they mean the same thing, the first suggests that Frederick could be one of several of my sons, while the second implies that he is my one and only son. Once again, if we wish to be quite clear about who invented the whoopee cushion, we need a more positive identification, perhaps:

My youngest son Frederick . . .

or

My only son, Frederick . . .

These are perhaps light-hearted instances of comma problems but occasionally a meaning that depends upon the presence or absence of a comma can be of great significance. Take the following statement, first with the comma, and then without it. We are forced to ask: who has the violent seizures caused by thunder, the invalid or the herdsman?

He looks after a herd of cows owned by a chronic invalid who constantly yells at him (,) and has seizures of the most violent kind whenever there's thunder about.

The Pause That Refreshes:
The many functions of the comma

Thus far we've looked at how we use, misuse and abuse the humble comma. Now let's bring some order and positivism into the discussion by looking at the ways in which commas can help us express ourselves with clarity and elegance.

Its most common function is to separate words, phrases and groups of words in a sentence to render it understandable – to divide a sentence into easily assimilable bite-sized pieces. We soon learn to recognise that commas signal the ends of word groups, and because they are always used *within* sentences, that more is to follow.

That is the most basic function of the comma, but there are many others:

• *Setting apart names and persons*:

Are you going to meet him, John?
That, ladies and gentlemen, is the situation.

I say, you over there, please keep quiet!
Of course you can do it, you dimwit!
Listen, Fred, I've had enough.
Darling, don't you think you've gone too far?

- *Itemising words*:

Please place all towels, costumes, clothing,
footwear and valuables in the lockers.

- *Itemising word groups*:

Please place any articles of clothing, swimming
and sporting equipment, personal belongings,
but not money and jewellery, in the lockers.

- *Enclosing additional thoughts or qualifications*:

The occasion was, on the whole, conducted with
all suitable solemnity.
The class thought it was, arguably, one of his
finest novels.

- *Setting apart interjections*:

Look, I've had enough!
Oh, have it your way, then!
Stop, or I'll call the police.
Blimey, isn't the beach crowded?

- *Indicating pauses before direct speech*:

Phyllis turned abruptly and said, 'If that's the way
you feel about me, then why don't you go?'

- *Introducing questions*:

You *are* going, aren't you?

- *Emphasising points of view*:

  Naturally, I'll look after her.
  Of course, he fully deserves the prize.
  Anyway, I won't be going to the concert.

- *Setting off comparative or contrasting statements*:

  The taller they are, the farther they fall.
  The more he adored her, the less she cared.

- *Reinforcing statements*:

  She's ill because she won't eat, that's why!
  It'll come right in the end, surely.

Like little fleas that have lesser fleas upon them, these
functions can be subdivided, but we'll resist the
temptation. However there are some comma
applications worth further and more detailed
attention.

Using Commas With Adjectives

Using commas to form lists of nouns and proper nouns
is, as we've seen, quite straightforward. We don't say,
for example,

Bill and Jean and Marcus and Chloe went out
riding.

or

Bill Jean Marcus and Chloe went out riding.

but

Bill, Jean, Marcus and Chloe went out riding.

A similar group of *adjectives*, used to modify a noun or proper noun, requires a bit more care. See if you can work out, in these two sentences, why one has the adjectives separated by commas, and the other does not:

> The night resounded with a loud, chilling, persistent ringing.
> It was a large brick Victorian mansion.

The reasons are embodied in two seemingly simple rules:

- Where the adjectives (or other modifiers) define separate attributes or qualities (*loud, chilling, persistent*), they are best separated by commas.

- Where the adjectives work together to create a single image (*large, brick, Victorian*), the commas are best avoided.

These rules, however, are notoriously difficult to apply, and the application of sense and common sense is often needed. That late, great grammarian Sir Ernest Gowers was never too bothered about commas between adjectives, quoting as equally correct,

- 'a silly, verbose, pompous letter'

and

- 'a silly verbose pompous letter'

and adding that the commas in this case merely added emphasis to the adjectives.

Nevertheless, comma placement between adjectives can lead to ambiguity. See how a comma here can make all the difference to the meaning:

A pretty smart young woman.
A pretty, smart young woman.

In the first example, the adjective *pretty* attaches itself to the next adjective *smart,* to mean something between 'fairly smart' and 'very smart'; moreover it makes no reference to the young woman's appearance. The second example means that here we have an attractive young woman who is also smart.

One way to look at this ticklish problem is to imagine an *and* between the adjectives; if an *and* can be inserted and still make sense, then a comma should be substituted:

Tracy was a young *and* exciting photographic model.
Tracy was a young, exciting photographic model.

Now let's look at a sentence where inserting an *and* would be plainly silly:

Tracy was a beautiful young model.
Tracy was a beautiful *and* young model.

This sentence, with or without a comma between *beautiful* and *young,* would mean the same thing, but the comma would be an irritant to eye and ear and mind because it splits what should be a single image: *beautiful young.*

But don't become obsessional about grammatical exactitude in this matter where your eye for style is perhaps more relevant. Here's a construction of five adjectives which could be written without commas but which I prefer to write with one:

She wore the eye-catching, Parisian blue silk designer dress with extraordinary flair.

The Oxford, or Final Comma

The Times curtly advises its journalists to 'avoid the so-called Oxford comma: x, y and z instead of x, y, and z.' What this means is that

> He spoke to Edith, Lesley, Bunty and Samantha.

is preferred to

> He spoke to Edith, Lesley, Bunty, and Samantha.

This is good advice: the final comma before *and* in a list is now outmoded – unless there is the possibility of ambiguity:

> The colours are red, white and blue.

Does this mean three separate colours, or two – red, and white and blue in some sort of combination? It's possible, so it would be a good idea to follow white with a comma to avoid confusion.

Or take this example:

> The drinks she liked most were lemonade, cream soda and dandelion and burdock.

For the uninitiated, there could be a drink called *cream soda and dandelion* and another called *burdock*. So, again, to make it perfectly clear:

> The drinks she liked most were lemonade, cream soda, and dandelion and burdock.

Commas With Adverbs and Adverbial Phrases

It has been customary to enclose adverbs and adverbial phrases with commas:

You are, nevertheless, guilty of the first charge.

Here are some more adverbs and adverbial phrases that traditionally have required commas:

however, indeed, in fact, needless to say, no doubt, incidentally, anyway, for example, on the contrary, as we have seen, of course

But the wisdom nowadays is to dispense with such commas if the meaning of the statement remains clear without them:

You are nevertheless guilty of the first charge.

There are plenty of occasions, however, (notice I've used the traditional enclosing commas to emphasise a reservation) where commas around adverbs are vital. A good example:

The hospital informed us that both victims were, happily, recovering.

Without the enclosing commas we'd be led to believe that the victims were not only recovering but having the time of their lives!

Commas are also needed for sentences beginning with adverbs:

Curiously, the two had never met.
Ironically, they discovered they were sisters.

and also for sentences containing adverbial clauses:

Looking scared, Peter peered out of the window.
Peter, *not given to heroics*, smartly lowered his
head.

The difference in meaning caused by enclosing an
adverb with commas or dispensing with them can be
extremely subtle, and you are urged to put reason
before rule and 'listen' to your sentence to see if it
carries the sense you've intended. Can you detect the
slight but discernible shift in meaning in the second
of these two statements?

The food is vastly expensive; nevertheless, I'll
always go there when I can afford it.
The food is vastly expensive; nevertheless I never
pass up the chance to eat there.

In the first, the writer emphasises his determination
to revisit the restaurant despite the expense, while in
the second, *nevertheless* is not emphasised and thus
gives the impression that the writer is rather
cheerfully casual about it all. Less subtle is the
following statement given as evidence by a naval
officer at a maritime court:

'I decided on an alteration of course.'

When the proceedings of the court were published,
the traditionally-trained compositor had taken it
upon himself to insert an inferred comma:

'I decided on an alteration, of course.'

Other Problem Comma Placements

Here's an example where commas enclose verbs to help
guide you through an otherwise tortuous sentence:

In the daytime, *sleeping*, she was adorable, but at nights, *howling continually*, she was a monster.

In much the same way a clarifying comma is usually required between two conjunctions:

She asked *whether*, *if* the register was available, she might look up her family records.

You can see the logic of using commas in complex sentences such as those above. Here's yet another example; this time with commas separating prepositions:

The helicopter hovered in, around, over and finally through the eerie pink cloud.

In this brief miscellany, it's worth mentioning one of the most common instances of the misplaced comma: the comma placed before an *and* when it should be placed after:

WRONG: He glanced up at the house, and abruptly closing his book, leapt up from the lawn.
RIGHT: He glanced up at the house, and, abruptly closing his book, leapt up from the lawn.
RIGHT: He glanced up at the house and, abruptly closing his book, leapt up from the lawn.

You can see the logic in this, can't you? But while the comma after *and* in sentences like the above have stayed with us, the convention of preceding *that* with a comma has virtually been abandoned:

What thing is it, that the less it is the more it is feared? (a bridge)
He made the observation, that the term 'back to square one' originated in the *Radio Times*.

Commas as Parenthesis

Now we come to what I think is the most interesting, but also perhaps the most contentious, use of commas – to parenthesise (or bracket) relevant but not essential matter from the main part of a sentence:

The wild hyacinths (which are at the height of their season) tint the woods with a blue mist.

The essential message here is *The wild hyacinths tint the woods with a blue mist* – but we've suddenly had a further thought – *which are at the height of their season* that we'd like to include in the same sentence. Sometimes we enclose such thoughts in parenthesis (brackets – more on these later) but mostly we use two far more convenient and less disruptive commas:

The wild hyacinths, which are at the height of their season, tint the woods with a blue mist.

Remember, won't you, to add the second comma; leaving it out is a very common and sloppy practice:

WRONG: He wrote the year's biggest bestseller, *Storm Over Jackdaw Bay* in just over three months.

RIGHT: He wrote the year's biggest bestseller, *Storm Over Jackdaw Bay*, in just over three months.

We even use commas to parenthesise items like dates:

On July 4, 1977, we had our first Independence Day party.

This parenthesising quality of commas is so strong that the effect of separating subordinate matter can be achieved with a single comma. Here are three

47

versions of a statement the meaning of which remains the same; example **A** uses a pair of enclosing commas, while **B** and **C** do the same job with one:

A The lawn grass mixture, however fast it might grow, turns brown with the slightest drought.
B However fast it might grow, the lawn grass mixture turns brown with the slightest drought.
C The lawn grass mixture turns brown with the slightest drought, however fast it might grow.

In each case, *however fast it might grow* is effectively separated from the main thrust of the sentence.

Now that we've seen how commas are used to isolate subordinate statements, what are these commas doing in this sentence?

The two lead actors, who appear in *Grease*, won their respective roles after a gruelling eight years in musicals.

The two enclosing commas here are telling us that 'who appear in *Grease*' is non-essential information. But if you rewrite the sentence without it, it doesn't make sense – we don't know who the lead actors are or what they are doing. In fact 'who appear in *Grease*' is called a defining or restrictive phrase – one that identifies, modifies or qualifies its subject. So the sentence should read:

The two lead actors who appear in *Grease* won their respective roles after a gruelling eight years in musicals.

There really is no choice in this matter, and to get it wrong is certain to leave any reader floundering in a swamp of ambiguity and confusion.

This two-comma convention allows us to determine instantly what, in any sentence, is essential to the subject of the sentence and what is not. To drive this important point home, follow the reasoning in the following examples:

A Salmon, which are migratory, are undoubtedly the king of British river fish.

B Salmon which can leap heights of up to fifteen feet scoop furrows in upstream reaches to deposit their spawn.

In **A** *which are migratory* is an interesting fact but non-essential, so it is in effect parenthesised by commas. The sentence is about **all** salmon as a genus – no restrictions or exceptions – which are all migratory.

In **B**, however, we are not discussing **all** salmon, but only those super-sexed specimens which can leap up waterfalls fifteen feet high to lay their spawn in the shallows. Because *which can leap heights of up to fifteen feet* is the essential information by which we identify these particular salmon, no commas are called for.

Here's another pair of examples which demonstrates how the two comma rule, wrongly applied, can lead to ambiguity:

A Women from Liverpool, who can't swim, are likely to drown.

B Women from Liverpool who can't swim are likely to drown.

In **A** the writer appears to be insulting the good women of Liverpool in a tart little aside by claiming none of them can swim. In **B**, though, the phrase *who can't swim* defines just those women who could be in danger of drowning.

For fear of labouring this point we will consider only one more case, which again provides the opportunity for misunderstanding:

A   The insurance policy which I took out in 1980 will take care of the mortgage.

B   The insurance policy, which I took out in 1980, will take care of the mortgage.

What do these two statements mean? **A** clearly means that the policy taken out in 1980 is the one that will take care of the mortgage; it also gives the impression that this is not the only policy I have. **B**, on the other hand, by relegating the facts about this particular policy as unimportant, implies strongly that this is the *only* insurance policy I have.

To sum up then:

- Where a phrase or clause does not define or qualify the subject, indicate that it is non-essential matter by isolating it with commas.

- Where a phrase or clause defines or qualifies the subject, weld it to the subject by omitting the commas.

The Semicolon

It's a common problem: whether to first tackle the colon and then the semicolon; or the other way around. The colon was first on the scene, after all, and at first sight it looks more straightforward and easier to use than its younger sibling. But for the rather dubious reason that semicolons considerably outnumber colons in everyday use, grammarians prefer it this way, so let's parrot Partridge.

It's easy to define a semicolon as half a colon, but that wouldn't be an entirely correct description. To say that a semicolon is a pause somewhere between a strong comma and a weak full stop is nearer the mark, but this still lacks precision. The fact is, using semicolons involves nuances of judgement and style which evade definition.

Consider the following statement in four formats:

He was once a dunce at maths. Now he is a mathematics professor.
He was once a dunce at maths now he is a mathematics professor.
He was once a dunce at maths, now he is a mathematics professor.
He was once a dunce at maths but now he is a mathematics professor.

As we have seen in the previous chapter, the second and third examples are grammatically wrong. There's nothing wrong with the first, except that it's a mite juvenile; the two statements scream to be joined! As for the fourth, hitching the statements together with the conjunction *but* (or *and, although* or *whereas*) is in danger of giving the resulting sentence a different emphasis than that intended.

The statement clearly implies that it is something of a surprise that the dunce became a professor. What punctuation device will project this irony? A semicolon, that's what:

He was once a dunce at maths; now he is a mathematics professor.

Done! The semicolon here not only links two independent but related sentences (which a comma can't do without a conjunction) but it also emphasises an incongruity as a bonus.

Even some experienced writers admit to having never completely mastered the semicolon, finding it the most difficult punctuation mark to use correctly. Some, like George Orwell and T. E. Lawrence, actually developed a hatred for it; in one of his novels, *Coming Up for Air* (1939) Orwell managed to exclude the semicolon altogether. Grammarians became so concerned for the future of the mark at one point that a Society for the Preservation of the Semicolon was founded.

The Functions of Semicolons

Semicolons are capable of a number of separate grammatical and stylistic tasks:

A   To join words, word groups and sentences
B   To separate word groups that already contain commas
C   To restore order in sentences already replete with commas
D   To separate and emphasise related antithetical ideas or statements
E   To provide a pause before adverbs such as *therefore, so, however,* etc.

Using Semicolons to Join Words, Word Groups and Sentences

Occasionally we find ourselves writing a long sentence with too many connecting words like *and, but* and *also* with the danger of getting into an impossible tangle. One solution is to recast the long sentence into two or more shorter ones. On the other hand you might feel that your thoughts flow more logically in a single sentence. Here's an offending sentence:

The history of the semicolon and colon is one of confusion because there are no precise rules governing their use and, furthermore, many writers would argue that both points are really stylistic rather than parenthetical, and that they can easily be replaced by commas, full stops or dashes, and there the argument rests.

There's nothing grammatically wrong with this effort, but it is unwieldy and unappealing to both eye and mind.

Now see how semicolons ease our passage through the mass of facts:

> The history of the semicolon and colon is one of confusion; there are no precise rules governing their use; many writers argue that both points are really stylistic rather than parenthetical and that they can easily be replaced by commas, full stops or dashes; and there the argument rests.

It is true that no precise rules govern the use of the semicolon. Here, finally, is what a writer of the 'snappy prose' persuasion might produce, and there is nothing wrong with it, either:

> The history of the semicolon and colon is one of confusion. There are no precise rules governing their use. Many writers argue that both points are really stylistic rather than parenthetical, and that they can easily be replaced by commas, full stops or dashes. And there the argument rests.

The use of semicolons to join single words is rarely called for, but here for the record is an example:

> Birth; life; death – three certainties in an uncertain world.

Using Semicolons to Separate Word Groups Containing Commas

Any sentence that is essentially a list should be crystal clear and readily readable. Most lists adequately separate the items with commas, but sometimes the items themselves are groups containing commas and require semicolons for clarity. Here are a couple of examples which demonstrate how handy semicolons can be:

> Those present included Mr and Mrs Allison and their daughters Sarah, Megan and Sue; the Smith twins, Reg and Paul; Joyce, Helen and Bill Hobson; etc.

> The line-up consisted of Bix Beiderbecke, cornet; Al Grande, trombone; George Johnson, tenor sax; Bob Gillette, banjo; Dick Voynow, piano, and Vic Moore on drums.

Semicolons Can Restore Order to a Sentence Suffering From 'Comma Riot'

Here's a longish and reasonably accomplished sentence spoiled by 'comma riot':

> His main aims in life, according to Wilma, were to achieve financial independence, to be powerfully attractive, not only to women but in particular to rich ladies, to eat and drink freely without putting on weight, to remain fit, vital and young-looking beyond his eightieth birthday and, last but not least, to not only read, but fully understand, Stephen Hawking's *Brief History of Time*.

The writer almost gets away with it, but in my view some longer pauses are called for and at least three of the eleven commas should be upgraded to semicolons:

> His main aims in life, according to Wilma, were to achieve financial independence; to be powerfully attractive, not only to women but in particular to rich ladies; to eat and drink freely without putting on weight; to remain fit, vital and

young-looking beyond his eightieth birthday and, last but not least, to not only read but fully understand Stephen Hawking's *Brief History of Time*.

You'll notice that the final two commas have been dropped and that with some of the thoughts separated by longer pauses the sentence achieves greater clarity and a more attractive rhythm.

Using Semicolons to Administer Mild Shocks

We've already had an example of how a semicolon can be placed to emphasise contrast and incongruity, but here are two more. For a woman to say,

I loved the hostess but thought it was a pity about her dress.

would be fairly pedestrian, and certainly lacking in feminine acuity. Here's what she might wish she'd said with the adroit use of a mental semicolon:

I loved the hostess; pity about the dress.

And secondly:

Bill claimed he'd eat anything; the chocolate coated ants were another matter.

Using Semicolons to Provide Pauses Before Certain Adverbs

There are certain adverbs and conjunctions which require a preceding pause, but one longer and stronger than that provided by a comma. Look at this example:

| WITH A COMMA | It was a beautiful car, moreover it was economical to run. |
| WITH A SEMICOLON | It was a beautiful car; moreover it was economical to run. |

You can see and hear that need for a substantial pause before *moreover*, can't you? A comma is wrong on both grammatical and rhetorical accounts. Here's another example; read it and note your instinctive pause before *nevertheless*:

> Joe claimed he'd beaten the bookies on every race; nevertheless he was broke as usual when he left the track.

Watch out for *therefore, however, besides, also, consequently, furthermore, hence, consequently* and *subsequently*; in many constructions they will require a preceding semicolon.

Semicolon pauses were once required for words like *so* and *then*, but now a comma suffices:

> I was zonked; so I went off to bed.
> I was zonked, so I went off to bed.

A Semicolon Self-test

Just to prove to yourself that you've grasped the principles of using semicolons, try these exercises. The corrected, or I should say recommended, versions will be found on page 111. Some of the examples will need recasting while one or two invite you to choose between commas and semicolons.

1 Everyone is wary of the cliff; the face of which has weathered alarmingly.

2 The couple scarcely knew anyone, and were slow to form friendships; having little enthusiasm for new faces.

3 It should be stressed that Stephanie's behaviour is unacceptable, it should be brought to her notice immediately.

4 The Austen household consisted of a cook, laundress, two maids and a butler, a groom and watchman and a head gardener and under-gardener.

5 Having lost his job in the recession, having had the ill-luck to lose his home and possessions to the bank, having, on top of everything, his wife leave him, Patrick was perhaps justified in feeling bitter.

(*For comment and answers, see page III*)

Trouble With Your Colon?

The history of the colon is brief: one of the first punctuation marks, dating from the Middle Ages, it virtually disappeared during the nineteenth century, only to be rescued from oblivion in the twentieth. Now, as we approach the twenty-first, it is under threat from the dash.

It is, therefore, a mark easily tossed aside, and many people write passable prose without ever feeling the need to use it. So why bother?

Well, you can cook without salt, too, or wear shoes without socks or stockings. Just as some relatively minor details can enrich your quality of life, so can the colon enhance the quality of your writing.

In fact the colon is a versatile workhorse, and many colon-scoffers are stopped in their tracks when confronted with the range of its functions.

But, first, there are two useful points to remember about colons:

- The difference between a semicolon and a colon is not a difference in weight or force; the two marks are mostly used for quite different purposes

- A colon is never followed by a capital letter, except with proper nouns: Emma, Ford Motor Co, etc.

Functions of the Colon

So far in this chapter I've used three colons, each for a different purpose. Here's a comprehensive list of the ways in which we can use them:

1 To point the reader's attention forward
2 To introduce a list
3 To present an explanation or example
4 To introduce direct speech
5 To present a conclusion
6 To introduce a subtitle
7 To substitute for a conjunction
8 To introduce a quotation
9 To introduce a question
10 To link contrasting statements

There are a few more functions explained at the end of this chapter, but, meanwhile, here are some examples of the colon in everyday use.

To Point the Reader's Attention Forward

In this role the colon acts as a pointing finger, as if to warn the reader about a statement ahead: '*Wait for it . . . here it comes!*' Or, in the more eloquent words of the grammarian Henry Fowler, its function is 'that of delivering the goods that have been invoiced in the preceding words'. The 'goods' might be a conclusion, a list, a summary or a contrasting statement:

> Maddeningly beautifully, honey-voiced, overwhelmingly generous, owner of three luxury homes: she was an object of desire to any man.

To Introduce a List

This is perhaps where colons are most commonly used:

> The hotel had everything: pool, sauna, Jacuzzi, gym, hairdresser, tanning booths and even a dietician.

To Present an Explanation or Example

> The beleaguered bank closed its doors after three days: not surprising when you saw the list of directors.

Introductory words and phrases such as *example* (and *e.g.*), *namely* and *as follows* are often followed by colons:

> There are three reasons why Lainston House near Winchester is an outstanding restaurant, namely: excellent cuisine, beautifully restored interiors, and super-attentive staff.

To Introduce Direct Speech

Although most stylists insist that commas are the correct marks to introduce direct speech with (see the chapter on **Commas** page 30), the use of colons today hardly earns a frown:

The mayor strode up to the platform, opened his notes and glared at the assembly: 'You have not come here tonight just to listen to me,' he growled.

To Present a Conclusion

Eighty-five years in the business suggested to him there was only one certainty in life: the inevitability of change.

To Introduce a Subtitle

In publishing, the colon is conventionally used to separate a subtitle from the main title:

Men at War: An Introduction to Chess
Gilbert White: Observer in God's Little Acre

To Substitute for a Conjunction

In the following example the writer preferred the punchier colon to a choice of conjunctions such as *and* or *but*:

Rodriguez downed him with a left hook that came from nowhere: Hayman did not get up.

To Introduce a Quotation

Rachel's thoughts were neatly summed up by Swift: 'That flattery's the food of fools; Yet now and then your men of wit will condescend to take a bit.'

To Introduce a Question

The essential question is simply this: did she or did she not seduce Sir Timothy?

To Link Contrasting Statements

In this role the colon steps into the ring with the
semicolon, which also has the ability to
administer a mild shock. The choice is, as these
examples illustrate, a matter of taste:

She cooks: I eat.

Jeremy had only one small fault: he was an
inveterate liar.

His love affair with his son's school, its history,
its achievements, its discipline and its crumbling
charm would have endured for ever but for one
small point: the £9,000 yearly fees.

Misuse of the Colon

Perhaps because many people steer clear of colons,
the mark is infrequently misused. But abuse exists,
not least in newspapers, as these three examples attest:

The man was amazing and was able to play: the
piano, violin, double bass, trombone, clarinet
and drums.

This is of course a plain case of 'redundant colon'; if
you listen to the sentence you'll readily agree that it
reads better without any mark or pause after *play*.
This second example occurred in an article on
cherries in a national newspaper:

Today's English cherry, however, is likely to be
Canadian in origin, bred to be split-resistant and
grown on dwarf rootstocks: 11 or 12ft high.

Now this really is confusing, as the unnecessary colon
leads us to believe that the rootstocks are 11 or 12ft
high, which can hardly be described as 'dwarf'! What

is apparently meant is that the *entire* tree is 11 to 12ft high, in which case the sentence ought to be rewritten:

> Today's English cherry, however, is likely to be Canadian in origin, bred to be split-resistant and grown on dwarf rootstocks to achieve a total height of 11 or 12ft.

The final example is a piece of compressed journalese:

> The desperate Prime Minister was forced to axe Nadir victim Michael Mates despite telling him privately: you've done nothing wrong.

The writer has, I suppose, done nothing wrong, either; colons are versatile and optional marks. But the colon here is ill-fitting and the sentence is clumsy. Here is a suggestion for a rewrite:

> The desperate Prime Minister was forced to axe Nadir victim Michael Mates despite telling him privately, 'You've done nothing wrong'.

The Colon: Sundry Uses

In addition to all of the functions described so far, we haven't yet finished with this extremely useful mark. If you ever read a play, you'll invariably find it laid out like this:

> GEORGE: YOU'VE SAID ENOUGH!
> ANNA: I HAVEN'T EVEN STARTED ...
> GEORGE: ENOUGH, D'YOU HEAR ME!

Then there is the 'biblical' colon, separating chapter and verse (*Ecclesiastes 3:12*); the mathematical colon used to express ratios (*Male athletes outnumber females by 2:1*); and the time colon (*The train leaves at 12:45*) although this use is more usual in the US than in Britain. Americans are also inclined to use colons instead of commas when opening a letter:

Dear Reader:
             I think we have said about all there
is to say about the colon.

The Seductive Embrace of the Bracket

In our discussion of commas we saw how material could be parenthesised or set apart (the term *parenthesis*, via Latin from Greek, means 'an insertion beside') by placing it between two commas.

The sentence above is just such an example, except that instead of using a pair of commas we have used a pair of brackets, or more correctly, round brackets. And because these brackets are used solely for the purpose of *parenthesising*, they are commonly known as *parentheses* and the material captured between them is said to be in *parenthesis*. For the sake of simplicity, however, we will call a bracket a bracket.

If you look at that first sentence again, you will see that the brackets serve to set apart relevant matter which could, if you wished to be ruthless, be dropped altogether. If you did prune away those words, the sentence would still express the same thought with an uninterrupted flow. But by retaining the words (in parenthesis) the sentence, and the reader, gain from the additional information.

So what's the difference between parenthesising material between commas and between brackets? Generally, material within commas is still very much part of the sentence, and must observe the grammatical conventions of the sentence. Bracketed material, on the other hand, is rather more distanced from the main sentence. Brackets also release the writer from a lot of responsibility as the parenthesised material, leading a separate life as it were, is not required grammatically to match the sentence into which it is inserted. Neither capitals nor full stops are needed unless the enclosed material consists of one or more sentences. Thus, for many writers brackets are a Godsend; unfortunately these same writers are also prone to over-use them.

The bracket's embrace is seductive and extremely adaptable as the following catalogue of examples of usage will demonstrate.

ADDING INFORMATION	One of the earliest dictionaries which sets out to explain 'difficult terms' is that of Elisha Coles (London, 1685).
EXPLANATION	Unable to follow the French instructions and after nothing but trouble he returned the car (a Renault saloon) to the garage.
AFTERTHOUGHT	During the tour they visited at least a dozen cities and towns (but why not, we wondered, Paris and Marseilles?) in just ten days.
CLARIFICATION	The directive stated quite clearly (page 15, second paragraph) that the premises would close from March 1.

COMMENT	The women of Brayville were refused admission (why?) earlier that day.
ILLUSTRATION	The candidate spent far too long discussing irrelevancies (15 minutes on the price of footwear; another ten on the evils of tax havens) with the result that most of his listeners walked out.
REMARKS IN CONFIDENCE	We're finally leaving here on Thursday (Oh, God, I can't wait!) and I'll write as soon as I can.
INDICATING OPTIONS	Your document(s) will be forwarded to the prospective employer.
EXPRESSING DOUBT	According to the magazine, Priscilla was always the cleverest, sportiest, most-liked (?) girl in her class.

You will see that all these examples conform in two important ways:

- Take the parenthesised matter away and the sentences flow on freely.
- The parenthesised matter assumes its own punctuation, separate from that of the surrounding sentence.

Abusing the Bracket

Is it possible to misuse or abuse such a straightforward, easy-to-use punctuation mark? Misuse is relatively rare, but abuse abounds. How often do we see brackets bulging with the contents of a fifty- or sixty-word paragraph, which is so long that by the time we get to the end of it we've lost the drift of the main sentence? If you find yourself writing a parenthesised statement longer than a dozen words, stop and think about restructuring the sentence.

Here's an example of another form of bracket abuse, although more stylistic than grammatical. It occurred, of all places, in a review of a book about punctuation:

'Admittedly, punctuation has changed little since the middle of the 16th century, when the widespread dissemination of typefaces among the printers of Europe began to make standardisation possible. (The semicolon as we know it had taken root about 1494; the comma nearer 1520; the apostrophe in 1529.)'

So, what's wrong with that? For one thing, I think it is difficult to justify the parenthesis anyway. The review ran in *The Times* which says in its style guide: 'Like capitals and dashes they [brackets] look ugly in a column of type and should be avoided wherever possible'. And, secondly, a bracketed afterthought isn't the most elegant way with which to close a sentence or a paragraph. Here's a rewrite, without the brackets:

'Admittedly, punctuation has changed little since the middle of the 16th century; the semicolon as we know it had taken root about 1494, the comma nearer 1520 and the apostrophe in 1529; after which the widespread dissemination of typefaces among the printers of Europe began to make standardisation possible.'

Even less justified is the following bracketed appendage which, again, occurred in a book review.

You can see immediately that the brackets are wholly redundant:

> '*Killing Ground* is the story of the Battle of the Atlantic, a full-scale war, with no rules and no mercy. (It is also the story of the destroyer, HMS *Gladiator*, and her company.)'

The Square Bracket

Square brackets are not angular forms of round brackets; they have a different function entirely. Unlike matter within round brackets, words enclosed in square brackets are not intended to be part of a sentence, but as an editorial or authorial insert:

> 'It was a matter of opinion that if offered the position, he [Professor Brandmeyer] would most likely refuse it on moral grounds.'

This sentence came at the end of a long paragraph; the professor's name had been mentioned at the beginning, but other names and a lot of discussion followed so that the reference to *he* was in danger of being misunderstood. The editor therefore inserted the name [Professor Brandmeyer] in square brackets to remove all doubt and also to indicate that the intervention was the editor's and not the author's.

One of the most common uses of square brackets is to enclose the adverb *sic* (from the Latin *sicut*, meaning 'just as') to indicate that incorrect or doubtful matter is quoted exactly from the original:

> Pink and yellow concubines [sic] climbed in great profusion up the trellis.

> The dog ran up to the car, whelping [sic] loudly and incessantly.

Square brackets are mostly confined to the domains of publishing and academia. The typewriter keyboard held only round brackets but as the word processor possesses both forms be prepared for a rash of bracketmania [square variety].

A Dash to the Rescue

The dash is a much maligned mark. Newspaper style guides are quite stroppy on the subject. 'Dashes are a bad habit,' intones one, 'often used to pursue a line of thought that the writer cannot be bothered to construct some other way.' Grammar purists decry the substitution of the dash for the colon.

But in the last decade or two the dash has attracted a growing band of defenders. '*It's the most exciting and dramatic punctuation mark of them all,*' claim some. Others admire its flexibility and its disdain for rules. It is a bit of a larrikin and a lot of fun in the often po-faced world of punctuation.

One of its defenders is the formidable Eric Partridge who, in a bold exposition in his *Usage and Abusage*, pronounces full grammatical health (and who could doubt him) on all these versions of the same statement:

BRACKETS	He was (God forgive him!) a scoundrel.
COMMAS	He was, God forgive him!, a scoundrel.
SEMICOLONS	He was; God forgive him!; a scoundrel.
COLONS	He was: God forgive him!: a scoundrel.

Partridge did, however, have the grace to admit to some discomfort with the comma, semicolon and colon versions, before commending the version with dashes:

DASHES   He was – God forgive him! – a scoundrel.

It doesn't take too much grammatical nous to see that the statement using dashes is the strongest, most dramatic and least fussy of them all.

So while agreeing that the dash has versatility (two dashes can *interrupt* a sentence – as they are doing now – while one can *extend* a sentence – like this) and respectability, it can also be a trap. Too many dashes can lead to writing that jars and irritates, both visually and mentally. I hesitate to impose a rule about dashes, but here's some good advice: don't use dashes in adjoining sentences, and restrict their use to a pair per page. And try not to use them as all-purpose marks – variety is the spice of punctuation, too.

Dashes for Parenthesis

The earlier example:

He was – God forgive him! – a scoundrel.

is a good example of a pair of dashes being used to parenthesise a statement, and this usage is growing by the day. You could take just about any example of parenthesising brackets and substitute dashes, and today few would object. The following sentence could be constructed using brackets, but what's wrong with dashes?

The dogs are so passive – they are impossible to goad or excite – that the breed makes the ideal children's pet.

While few forget to insert an enclosing bracket, many

writers fail to add the second dash. If you don't
believe me, here's the grammar authority G. V. Carey,
from his *Mind The Stop* (1939):

> No wonder that in some matters the dash has
> fallen into disrepute; but I still maintain that, if
> kept in its place – and I make one here for luck,
> it is a very useful stop.

Unfortunately Mr Carey's luck ran out in this sentence
because he forgot to complete his parenthesis with a
second dash between *luck* and *it*, where he has
incorrectly and inconsistently placed a comma.

The Versatile Dash

Here are some instances in which you can creatively
– and legitimately – use dashes. The first of these is
perhaps also the most common: in substituting for
colons.

LINKING DEVICE	Mrs Sims had four small daughters – Poppy, Iris, Pansy and Petal.
	On that particular evening, Malcolm had one overwhelming passion – to eat his way through the entire menu.
AS A PAUSE	Everyone expected the speaker to be controversial – but not to the extent of swearing at the chairwoman and falling off the stage.
SIGNALLING SURPRISE OR PARADOX	A straight line is the shortest distance between two points – when you're sober.

Then the adhesive gave way, the beard came adrift and Santa Claus was revealed as – Aunt Mildred!

David Marquand is one of those rare commodities in British politics – an intellectual.

INDICATING DISRUPTION AND INTERRUPTION	'There will be, of course, er – a small charge, but—'
	'You never mentioned a charge – not a word – there's no way—'
	'I'm sorry. It was – you know—' 'Sorry! It's too late—' etc., etc.
SEPARATING LISTS	She assembled all the ingredients – flour, sugar, eggs, salt, lard and raisins – and started on the pudding.
AFTER-THOUGHTS	They babbled on, delighted at seeing the rare parakeet – I didn't see so much as a feather.

The Dash in Sentence Construction

For some examples of the use of the dash by a master of the language, here are some excerpts from *Love and Death in a Hot Country* by Shiva Naipaul. First, see how he chooses to use a dash to introduce the subjects, and then a colon to set off a conclusion:

'Everything seemed more dramatic than ever – Aubrey, the woman he called his wife, himself, the hot square of garden: shadows whose actions and words he did not fully understand.'

Secondly, he prefers dashes to parenthesise, rather than commas:

> 'Dina had no idea what – if anything – was expected of her.'

And, again, a dash substitutes for a colon:

> 'Imagine a family – a family, if you wish, like my own.'

Finally, here's an ultra-long parenthetical passage I would not recommend anyone to attempt. But see how, after the closing dash, Naipaul cleverly repeats his opening phrase 'The surprising thing', so that the reader, whose attention might have drifted, is smartly reunited with the main sentence:

> 'The surprising thing about the imminent abandonment of the Constitution – that lengthy charter so top-heavy with ringing preambles, so glutinously coated with abstract principles of right and justice and obligation, so ribboned with guarantees to minorities and special interests, so honeycombed with promises of life and liberty and happiness for all, so stiff with austere legalism, so sweetened with the codes of civility, that Constitution painstakingly fabricated and assembled over several weeks in panelled, chandeliered halls and flourished in triumph at the climax – the surprising thing was not that it was about to be unceremoniously tossed out of the window but that it had taken such a comparatively long time for that to happen.'

Let us at last make peace with the dash.

Quotation Marks

Quotation marks or *inverted commas*? The former is correct because, with some minor exceptions, that is what they are used for: to enclose actual spoken words or quotations from other texts. The latter is a misnomer; if you look closely at these marks in any book or newspaper you will see that only the opening mark is inverted – that is, the tail of the tadpole is pointing up – while the closing mark is a normal raised or hanging comma or pair of commas. So we will be using the term *quotation marks* (or *quotes* for short) exclusively.

Another point about quotation marks is whether to use them singly or in pairs:

> Heather said flatly, 'I don't want to see him again.'
> Heather said flatly, "I don't want to see him again."

Newspapers and book publishers are divided on this. Some, like *The Sunday Times*, *The Times*, the *Independent* and the *Sun*, prefer double commas, while the *Observer* and the *Mail* opt for single quote marks. Among publishers, books issued by Secker & Warburg and Chatto & Windus have double quotes; books published by Penguin, Michael Joseph and Oxford University Press prefer single quotation marks. Generally, the trend is towards typographic simplicity and single marks.

Once you make the heroic decision about whether to use single or double marks, you need to be aware of the convention for enclosing a quote within a quote. If you're a single-quote writer, an additional quote within your first quote must be enclosed with double marks:

The sales assistant said, 'We only have them in grey and blue but yesterday my boss told me, "I don't know why they don't make them in other colours".'

If there is ever an occasion – and it should be a rare occasion – where a quotation contains a third quote within a second quote, the alternation would be single/double/single.

Quoting Direct Speech

Although the authorised version of the Bible is buzzing with speeches, dialogue and discussion it contains not a single quotation mark.

This would hardly do today. When we read a newspaper report or an interview or a novel we want to know when we're reading reported or interpolated speech and when we're reading words actually spoken. Quotation marks help us differentiate between the two forms:

Mr Murphy said that in his view the value of the pound would drop towards the end of the year. 'I also believe most European currencies will follow suit,' he added.

This tells us that the writer has summarised the first statement in his own words, and we have to accept that his summary is a correct version of what Mr Murphy said. With the second statement we should have no doubt about its accuracy because the quotation marks signal that the words are those actually spoken by Mr Murphy.

It is therefore essential to ensure that in quoted speech (or quoted text) the words enclosed by quotation marks are *exactly* those spoken. Not approximately, but *exactly*.

This is pretty fundamental, yet it is surprising how

many people, including some famous writers, get it wrong. The English expert J. E. Metcalf, who delighted in exposing the solecisms of the famous, loved to quote this errant passage from Jane Austen's classic novel, *Persuasion*:

> Sir Walter thought much of Mrs Wallis; she was said to be an excessively pretty woman, beautiful. 'He longed to see her. He hoped she might make some amends for the many plain faces he was continually passing in the streets . . .' Poor Sir Walter!

It's obvious that the quotes attributed to Sir Walter were not spoken by him (if they were, they would read: 'I long to see her. I hope she might make some amends . . .' etc.) so why did Jane use quotation marks? This and other lapses from *Persuasion* are among literature's more intriguing mysteries.

You can see endless possibilities for confusion, can't you? Look at these two almost similar sentences:

A Jones stated that 'he was innocent of the crime.'
B Jones stated that he was 'innocent of the crime.'

In **A**, Jones did not say 'I was innocent' but, 'he was innocent'. By this we have to assume that Jones, by referring to 'he', is talking about another person whom he says is innocent. In **B**, the words uttered by Jones – those enclosed in quotation marks – are 'innocent of the crime'. In the context of the sentence we assume that those words form an abbreviated version of his original statement:

C Jones stated, 'I am innocent of the crime.'

The difficulty is that, with Example **A**, the writer probably *did* mean to convey that Jones was innocent, but in misplacing the quotation marks he gives an ambiguous or incorrect version of the facts.

Despite everything you've read on speech quotation so far, the ground rules for punctuating speech are reasonably easy to follow. First, some random bits of advice:

- Make sure your reader knows who is responsible for the quoted statement. This is usually accomplished with what is called a *reporting clause*, which can introduce the statement or follow it or even divide it:

  1 *Jones stated*, 'I am completely innocent and I can easily prove it.'
  2 'I am completely innocent and can easily prove it,' *Jones stated*.
  3 'I am completely innocent,' *Jones stated*, 'and I can easily prove it.'

- Even if the quoted speech is limited to a single word, the same rules apply:

  The doctor described the patient's recovery as 'extraordinary'.

- With very long quotations that might extend to more than a paragraph, use only an opening quotation mark at the start of each paragraph. Use the closing quotation mark only at the very end of the quoted statement.

- It is usual to introduce quotations with a comma or a colon:

  Theodora sighed, 'I've felt so tired lately.'
  Theodora sighed: 'I've felt so tired lately.'

- When quoted speech is interrupted by a reporting

clause (see above) two rules apply. If the statement is interrupted at the end of a sentence it should be finished with a comma and resumed with a capital letter:

'I knew I'd seen that bird before,' said Gavin. 'It was a cormorant, wasn't it?'

But if the speech is interrupted within a sentence, it should be resumed in lower-case:

'Don't you agree,' asked Gavin, 'that the bird over there is a cormorant?'

- Don't forget to close your quotations.

None of this should present any difficulty. But there is one aspect of quotation punctuation that has somehow earned a reputation for being impenetrable: how to correctly close quotations.

How to Close Quotations

The problem is simply this. In the following example,

He then asked her, 'Do you think I'm drunk'?

do you place the question mark *outside* the direct speech quotation mark, or

He then asked her, 'Do you think I'm drunk?'

within the final quotation mark? The answer is that it depends on the relationship between the quotation and the sentence that contains it. The rule is – and pay attention, now! –

PUNCTUATION MARKS (FULL STOPS, COMMAS, QUESTION AND

EXCLAMATION MARKS ETC.) GO *INSIDE*
THE FINAL QUOTATION MARK IF THEY
RELATE TO THE QUOTED WORDS BUT
OUTSIDE IF THEY RELATE TO THE
WHOLE SENTENCE.

In the example above, the question mark relates only
to the quoted statement, 'Do you think I'm drunk?'
and so it rightly belongs *inside* the final quote mark.
But let's change the sentence slightly:

Should he have asked her, 'Do you think I'm drunk'?

I think you can see that now the question is an essential
part of the whole sentence. To be absolutely pedantic
about it, the sentence should properly be written like
this:

Should he have asked her, 'Do you think I'm
drunk?'?

Here you see that the quotation has its own question
mark *inside* the final quote mark, and the sentence
has its mark *outside*. But it looks pretty silly and
everyone accepts the convention that the inside
question mark can be dropped.
Here's another pair of examples:

I told her frankly, 'You're driving me around the
bend.'
He claimed she was driving him 'around the bend'.

In the first sentence the quoted statement 'You're
driving me around the bend' requires its own
punctuation, so the full stop goes *inside* the final quote
mark. In the second, the quotation 'around the bend'
is merely a fragment within the sentence and needs
no punctuation of its own, so the full stop goes *outside*
the final quote mark.

Here is a small collection of examples in which, if you follow the logic of their construction you will understand the punctuation:

1 'Did you speak just now?'
2 All he could manage to say was, 'It's about time!'
3 Harry came up to me and said, quite calmly, 'Hullo, John, I've had a sex change'!
4 Most critics praised the book: 'Is this one of the great comic creations of all time?' asked the *Evening Standard*.
5 Most critics praised the book, the *Evening Standard* asking, 'Is this one of the great comic creations of all time?'
6 'Are you going to the shops?' he asked. 'Or are you staying here?'
7 'I think I'll go out,' she said. 'The rain has stopped, thank goodness.'
8 'Are you,' he asked irritably, 'going to the shops or not'?

Most of these examples are self-explanatory, but here are some observations:

4 Many writers would find it hard to resist placing the question mark after *Standard*.
5 Theoretically, there should be a full stop outside the final quote mark, but convention allows it to be dropped.
6 There are two questions here, each requiring a question mark inside the final quote mark.
7 The same point applies; here there are two sentences, each requiring their own full stop.
8 With interrupted sentences the punctuation mark is placed outside the final quote mark. The question runs right through the sentence.

Americans Make It Easy

While they may be logical, some of the finer points of punctuation placement can be difficult to follow. However, there is a simple solution: move to the US, where they chuck logic out of the window. American practice – in books, newspapers, any kind of writing – is *always* to place the punctuation within quotation marks, no matter what. It may not be logical but it certainly has the merit of being consistent and absurdly easy to grasp.

UK In Britain, is it true to say, 'a question mark should be outside the final quotation mark'?

US In America, is it true to say, 'a question mark should be inside the final quotation mark?'

The sharper among you will know that both statements are true.

Other Functions of Quotation Marks

Most punctuation marks are multi-functional and quotation marks are no exception. Here are some other ways in which you can use them.

TO INDICATE TITLES

She said she'd seen the recipe in Delia Smith's 'Summer Collection'.

His favourite film was the Marx Brothers' classic, 'Duck Soup'.

TO IDENTIFY NICKNAMES AND SOBRIQUETS	Henry 'Rabbit Punch' Watson Beulah 'Bubbles' Henley-Howard Al 'Scarface' Capone.

TO IDENTIFY
NICKNAMES
AND
SOBRIQUETS

Henry 'Rabbit Punch'
Watson
Beulah 'Bubbles' Henley-
Howard
Al 'Scarface' Capone.

TO INDICATE
DOUBT,
CYNICISM OR
DISBELIEF

The hamburgers contained a
mix of liver, chicken parts
and 'beef'.

The councillor claimed that
all his supporters were
'students'.

The spokesman inferred that
lawyers were, on the whole,
charitable; but most people
would hesitate before
submitting themselves to the
mercy of 'charitable' lawyers.

TO INDICATE
THAT A WORD
OR PHRASE
SHOULD NOT
BE TAKEN
LITERALLY

Here's the headline from a
mail order advertisement:

**WHY ARE WE 'GIVING
AWAY' THIS NATION-
ALLY ADVERTISED
PYRAMID X100 FRESH
AIR IONISER FOR ONLY
£17.95?**

By the simple device of
enclosing the words *giving
away* in quotation marks the
headline was given a clean
(but grudging) bill of health
by the advertising standards
authorities.

Hassles with Hyphens

Did you ever see a stick walking? Or shudder at an ear splitting, or witness a room change? Obviously not, but just to make sure no one is hoodwinked we tend to hyphenate such words:

walking-stick; *ear-splitting*; *changing-room*

But not always. Among punctuation marks the hyphen is the most liable to alternate usage, illogical exceptions, variations and change. To people who like this sort of thing hyphens are the splice of life.

We've dealt with dashes and know that they are used, in various ways, to help us *construct sentences*. The hyphen helps us *construct words* to clarify meaning. At least that's what they set out to do.

Here are two similar newspaper headlines:

MAN EATING TIGER SEEN NEAR M1

MAN-EATING TIGER SEEN NEAR M1

The first headline suggests that some hungry fellow has decided to barbecue some choice jungle beast near a motorway, while the second could prove fatal should you be carelessly wandering around Luton. A hyphen has made all the difference.

In the same vein, *a little used car* (say a Mini) is not the same as *a little-used car* (eg a 6-litre Roller with only 3,000 miles on the clock). Nor is a *small businessman* necessarily a *small-businessman*, nor a *French polisher* a *French-polisher*. Or to quote a classic example, *superfluous hair-remover* may not be *superfluous-hair remover* – so beware.

The Evolutionary Hyphen

Hyphens are used to join, temporarily or permanently, two or more associated words. Sometimes this is done to create a useful compound word to describe something for which no word exists. Sometimes it is done to join two words to remove confusion (as with the examples opposite), or to act as a guide to pronunciation.

But one of the most interesting things about the hyphen is that, having done its job, it is often discarded and – presto! – a new word is born, unencumbered by punctuation. This process can take half a century or a decade. If you had lived in the 1950s you would have read words like *motor-car*, *tax-payer* and *man-power*. Today, as we know, they are single words without hyphens. And *today* itself was *to-day* in the nineteenth century; *tomorrow* was *to-morrow* and *yesterday* was *yester-day*.

This evolutionary process, however, is not consistent; some hyphenated compounds make it to respectability and some don't:

SEPARATE WORDS	HYPHENATED COMPOUND	UNIFIED WORD
son in law	son-in-law	(*unlikely*)
book seller	book-seller	bookseller
book keeper	book-keeper	(*unlikely*)
life like	life-like	lifelike

Sometimes the transition can be dated with great accuracy. In 1935 the mystery novelist Raymond Chandler coined the term *cover-up*; it lost its hyphen in the early 1970s to become the very useful word *coverup*, although you will still find the hyphenated version lingering in some dictionaries.

This inconsistency is, for most writers, a real hangup. To illustrate this, let's take a bunch of idiomatic 'hang' words, mostly from the past forty years or so, and see how they finish up in a typical dictionary – in this case the *Comprehensive Collins*.

ORIGINAL EXPRESSION	HYPHENATED COMPOUND	ACCEPTED WORD
hang up	hang-up	hangup (US)
hang glider	hang-glider	–
hang nail	hang-nail (1968)	hangnail
	hang-out (1972)	hangout
	hang-dog (1960)	hangdog
	hang-over (c1968)	hangover

The hyphen, as you can see, is a distinctly perverse little mark, and I suppose one shouldn't get too hung-up (?) about it. Half a century ago it was not uncommon to see *publichouse*; since then the single word has taken a reverse trip and is now *public house*, or 'pub' for short. But that's a rare case; for most hyphenated compounds the goal is to become a respectable word. Here are just a few of perhaps thousands of words that began life as two or more words linked with hyphens:

anticlimax, bloodyminded, businesslike, contradict, contraflow, earring, hindquarters, lampshade, lifelike, lifestyle, nightgown, nowadays, phoenixlike, postgraduate, posthumous, predeceased, predecessor, prehistoric, seaside, washbowl.

Hyphenated Marriages

Like marriage, hyphenation is a liberal institution;
hyphens are not too fussy about the words they link.
For example:

NOUN + VERB	*ham-fisted, hand-operated*
NOUN + ADJECTIVE	*director-general, postmaster-general*
ADVERB + VERB	*highly-praised*
VERB + PREPOSITION	*knock-down*

In many cases hyphens enter into marriages of
convenience; when, for instance, they act as guides
to pronunciation as with *co-operation*, *re-educate* and
re-establish.

Hyphens are also handy to avoid cases of 'letter
collision' which is visually confusing:

shell-like	is preferred to	*shelllike*
semi-illiterate	is preferred to	*semiilliterate*
anti-intellectual	is preferred to	*antiintellectual*
bell-like	is preferred to	*belllike*
de-ice	is preferred to	*deice*

Confoundingly, however, we seem to accept
unhyphenated words like *cooperative* and *coordination*.

Generally, hyphens are usual after the prefixes *ex-*
(ex-cop); *non-* (non-starter) and *self-* (self-employed).
They are not usually required after *anti-* (antifreeze);
counter- (counterweight); *co-* (coreligionist); *neo-*
(neoclassicism); *pre-* (prehensile) and *un-*
(unconditional). But unsurprisingly there are enough
exceptions to keep you on your toes: *neo-Nazi*, *co-respondent* (to distinguish it from *correspondent*) and
pre-empt. Watch out also for words with different
meanings like *recreation* and *re-creation*; *reform* and *re-form*; *relay* and *re-lay*.

And, finally on this topic, if you're combining a proper noun with a prefix, make sure you retain the capital letter: *pro-Tory*, *anti-Semitism*, *post-Thatcher*.

Other Functions of the Hyphen

Perhaps the most common function of the hyphen is the one we notice least: its role in syllabification. Syllabification? That's merely a fancy term for dividing a word at the end of a line:

> The young man's story contra-
> dicted the rather dubious tale told
> by the publican's wife.

In the not too distant past we saw rather more of these than we do today; modern typesetting technology with its ability to justify (align to the right) almost any line of print has almost obliterated the end-of-line hyphen.

Hyphens are essential for separating certain groups of words or names:

> The Conservative-Liberal Alliance
> The Paris-Washington Accord

and especially to make sense of double double-barrel examples like this, where the central dividing hyphen is not a dash but a 'long' hyphen:

> The event of the county season was the Hywell-Jones–Craig-Thomas wedding in May.

Hyphens are also trotted out for special effects:

> Blimey, it's c-c-c-cold in here!
>
> I'll repeat, my name is Smyth: S-M-Y-T-H, not Smith!

and are enormously useful for indicating fractions
(three-quarters, one-twentieth) and to abbreviate
dates (1939-45) and numbers (Vols. 21-25 inclusive).

A Hodgepodge of Hyphens

Here's a handy list of words and names that are
usually, but not always, hyphenated.

anti-abortion
bone-shaking, bull's-eye, brother-in-law
call-up, cat-o'-nine-tails, Coca-Cola, co-worker
daddy-longlegs, daughter-in-law, deaf-and-
   dumb, deep-sea fishing, do-it-yourself,
   double-cross, double-dealing, double-park,
   Dow-Jones
ear-splitting, ex-husband, ex-serviceman
face-saving, foot-and-mouth disease, forget-me-
   not, four-letter-word
get-together, give-and-take, good-for-nothing,
   good-looking
habit-forming, half-and-half, half-breed
   (virtually all words prefixed with 'half' carry a
   hyphen), helter-skelter, higgledy-piggledy,
   high-spirited, high-tech, hit-and-run
ill-advised, ill-timed, ill-treat, infra-red
jack-o'-lantern, jiggery-pokery, Johnny-come-
   lately
knock-for-knock, Ku-Klux-Klan
lady-in-waiting, large-scale, Land-Rover,
   Latter-day Saint, left-handed, light-headed,
   lily-white, long-distance runner/telephone call,
   loose-limbed, love-lies-bleeding, low-key
man-of-war, middle-aged, mother-in-law,
   mother-of-pearl, muu-muu
near-sighted, ne'er-do-well, non-starter
O-level, off-peak, off-putting, old-fashioned,
   one-night stand, out-of-doors

passer-by, penny-pinching, place-name, point-to-point, post-natal, price-fixing, pro-Irish
quick-tempered, quick-witted
right-handed, right-minded, rye-grass
St Martin-in-the-Fields, Saint-Saëns, sawn-off, set-aside, short-change, son-in-law, sub-lieutenant
test-tube baby, three-ring circus, tie-break, tip-off, T-shirt, trap-door spider, tutti-frutti, tut-tut
ultra-violet (but just as often **ultraviolet**)
vice-president
walk-on, walk-in, walkie-talkie, weather-beaten, well-known, well-thought-out, will-o'-the-wisp
X-ray

How Are Your Hyphens?

Here's a 30-second quiz to test your handling of hyphens. Which of the following options would you select? *Answers on page 112.*

1 (a) unself-conscious
   (b) unselfconscious
   (c) un-selfconscious

2 (a) ten-year-old child
   (b) ten-year-old-child
   (c) ten year old child
   (d) ten year old child

3 (a) all star cast
   (b) all-star cast

4 (a) fifty odd years
   (b) fifty-odd years

5 (a) There were six part- and four full-time employees
   (b) There were six part and four fulltime employees
   (c) There were six part-time and four full-time employees
   (d) There were six part-time and four fulltime employees

6 (a) ups and downs
   (b) ups-and-downs

Symbols
of Meaning

Questions and Exclamations

With the question and exclamation marks we enter
new punctuation territory. So far we've dealt with
units of space, separation and connection. The rest of
our punctuation marks are units of expression and
meaning.

The question mark and exclamation mark share a
common ancestry: both are developments of the full
stop. The question mark has the additional squiggle
atop of the stop, not unlike a *q* (for query?), while
the exclamation mark consists of a hanging stroke
pointing emphatically to the stop to make the reader
screech to a halt. Furthermore, as you will see, they
can slink into each other's backyard.

The Question Mark

A sentence that asks a question requires a question
mark, but indirect questions do not:

DIRECT QUESTION	'Are you going to the match?'
INDIRECT QUESTION	I asked him if he was going to the match.

One of the curious things about this mark is that you
have to reach the end of the sentence to be certain
that a question is being asked. This is not a problem
with short questions, but when you strike an

interminably long question, it can be. There is a case for placing the question mark at the beginning to signal to the reader that a question is coming, as they do in Spain. But enough of wishful thinking! Most of the time question marks close interrogative sentences, but not always:

His sister – who would have thought it? – passed all her A-level subjects with ease.

Most of us, most of the time, use question marks at the most simplistic level, and hardly anyone is the wiser. But for those who might wish to wield this mark with a little more panache, let's dig a little deeper into its usage. First of all, here is the mark being used in several ways:

INTERROGATIVE	*Are you from Canada?*
DECLARATIVE	*You're aware of the problem, aren't you?*
EXCLAMATORY	*Isn't this just fantastic?*
QUESTION TAG	*It's a great game, isn't it?*
REQUEST	*Would you let me know if either Monday or Tuesday next week is suitable?*

The first of these is, of course, the common, simple question that a child quickly learns how to use. The second type is not so simple; besides being a question it also carries overtones of frustration, curtness, even anger. The exclamatory question, appropriately named, could end with an exclamation mark and yet still remain a question. The tag question reinforces the first part of the sentence which might have been written *It's a great game?*; the tag makes sure the listener is aware that it is a question and invites an answer. The request question is the weakest of them all; requests typically beginning *Would you . . .* invariably finish with a stop:

Would you be good enough to ensure that, in future, cars and other vehicles belonging to non-staff are parked outside the gates.

This is half-question, half-demand, and both writer and reader know that a question mark would tend to destroy its authority.

The 'Semi'-question

Many people are troubled by this weasel-like quality. Look at these examples – all questions – and all seeming reasonably comfortable without the question mark:

You're not going to give in yet, I trust.
I wonder if I might borrow the car tomorrow.
I hope you're not calling me a liar.
Will you, in future, kindly refrain from calling
  me a liar in front of your mother.
Surely it's a matter for the police.

Such usage is plain laziness and should be discouraged. But there is an alternative, and that is to add force and expression to the question by substituting an exclamation mark:

You're not going to give in yet, I trust!
Are you completely mad!

In fact, some questions would look strange with a question mark:

How dare you?   How dare you!

Another manifestation of the absent question mark occurs frequently in newspaper sub-headlines. Here's a typical example from *The Sunday Times*:

'A hundred years after Freud, 50 after the development of potent psychiatric drugs, have our ideas of psychiatric care really progressed, asks Dr Anthony Clare.'

Not a question mark in sight! Why? Here's another example, from *The Times*:

'Why should allegations that go unchallenged in America be the subject of legal action in Britain, asks Roy Greenslade.'

Both sentences seem to be screaming for question marks – in the first after *progressed*, in the other after *Britain*. But if you look closer you will see that both sentences are novel forms of the indirect question which might be rewritten as:

Roy Greenslade asks why should allegations that go unchallenged in America be the subject of legal action in Britain.

While many writers are sloppily discarding the question mark, others, equally sloppy, have found a new use for it:

Many of the students claimed that they owed their success in life to the loving care (?) of the school's headmaster and his wife.

This usage – the 'snide' question mark to convey doubt, cynicism or sarcasm – is frowned on by grammar purists, and I think, this time, the purists are right. There are superior ways in which to express a hesitation to believe, that we all entertain at times:

Our neighbours were connoisseurs (?) of home-made country wines.

How much more telling is this vicious rewrite:

> Despite evidence to the contrary (ugh!) our
> neighbours kept insisting they were connoisseurs
> of home-made country wines.

Or the more economical but equally telling:

> Our neighbours were 'connoisseurs' of home-
> made country wines.

The Exclamation Mark

While not exactly indispensable, this device earns its
keep with a surprisingly wide range of uses.
Discouraged, if not banned, by modern newspapers
(where it is referred to as a 'startler', 'gasper',
'screamer' and by tabloid sub-editors as a 'dog's dick')
the reputation of the exclamation mark has suffered
not through any shortcomings on its part but because
of its over-use and misuse by writers.

The argument of the purists and stylists is that
whatever is expressed with the crutch of exclamation
marks can be better expressed by words alone. Really?
It's hard to imagine the following examples carrying
anything like the same force and feeling without the
screamers:

> Shut up! You bitch! What a mess! Damn!

Literature would undoubtedly be the poorer without
them. Barbara Cartland and Colette apart, most
works of fiction utilise the exclamation mark
judiciously, and for a number of functions:

CONVEYING	*You're out of your mind!*
ANGER, SCORN,	*You must be joking!*
DISGUST	*You've ruined everything!*

INDICATING IRONY AND REVERSE MEANING	*Thanks a lot!* *That's lovely, that is!*
UNDERLINING INSULTS AND EXPLETIVES	*You bastard!* *Shit!*
CONVEYING IRONIC TONE	*You're not so smart!* *And you thought we wouldn't win!* *Don't do anything I wouldn't do!*
COMMANDING	*Come here! Now!* *Get lost! And don't come back!*

With all these examples, the statements would be bland and colourless without the exclamation mark. And some would be completely meaningless:

Don't do anything I wouldn't do.

Substitute an exclamation mark for the full stop and the statement acquires a 'raised eyebrow' or 'wink, wink' tone to become the idiomatic invitation to have a good time.

Misuse of this mark undoubtedly contributes to its over-use. None of the following examples require it:

He wasn't the least bit smart!
She works as a receptionist at the surgery!
Peter thought he'd never pass!

Alas, such examples are only too common. Always think twice before using an exclamation mark, and think twenty times before using them in multiples:

Did Norma tell you how I got the sack from Burtons! Just for taking a lousy two-hour lunch-break last Friday! ! You can imagine just how I feel! ! !

From reading this, perhaps there was another reason why Norma's friend got the sack.

Catastrophes with Apostrophes

Early in 1993 there was a threat by British Airways to buy part of the Australian airline Qantas. Antipodean feelings ran high and a protest group erected a huge hoarding on the perimeter of Sydney International Airport:

PUBLIC NOTICE
NO BRITISH AIRWAYS OWNERSHIP OF
OUR **QANTAS**
PISS OFF POM'S

The highly (and internationally) visible admonition drew a barrage of complaints about the language on the big sign; not, however, objecting to the suggestion that the British should forthwith depart, but rather to the misuse of an apostrophe.

Hardly a day passes without the knowing among us having a chortle over some apostrophic clanger:

Lilie's, Anemone's and Mum's (London florist)
Fresh asparagu's (Edinburgh greengrocer)
Her's is a warm, informal home. (Newspaper interview)
Bargain Mens Shirt's (Market sign)
This school and it's playground closed over Easter (sign on gate at a Croydon school)

If we're honest, I think we all have to admit that there are times when we are forced to think hard about the use of apostrophes. So what's the problem?

The problem disappears the moment we accept that there are two kinds of apostrophes, and learn the difference between them. One kind indicates possession of something; the other kind indicates a contraction – a letter or letters left out of a word:

POSSESSIVE   Did you know Jack's car is a write-off?

CONTRACTION   Did you know Jack's had a bad accident?

In the first example the apostrophe tells us that the car belongs to Jack; that is a possessive apostrophe. In the second, the apostrophe tells us that something is left out; that *Jack's* is a shortened version of two or more words. We are expected to work out what this is and with experience we soon learn most of the accepted contractions. In this case *Jack's* is short for *Jack has*:

Did you know that Jack has had a bad accident?

Possessive Apostrophes

You may understand about possessive apostrophes a little better if you know how they came about. Before 1500, possession was indicated by a phrase which went something like 'the Bishop, his cassock'. In time, this was shortened to 'the Bishopis cassock' and then to the way it was pronounced, 'the Bishops cassock' but written 'the Bishop's cassock' with a raised comma to show that a letter had been dropped. And that is how the possessive (or genitive) apostrophe has come down to us today:

Joyce's house; Bill's lawnmower; a boy's bike; his uncle's car; her grandfather's clock

Possession, ownership or association can apply not only to people but also to things:

a good day's work; the company's policy; the tree's branches; a door's hinges

And the same goes for certain plural nouns:

men's trousers; children's toys; mice's tails

No problems there. But you'll notice that all the above examples have something in common: none of the possessor words or names end with an 's' – *Joyce, Bill, boy, uncle, grandfather, day, company, tree, door, men, children, mice*. So what's the big deal about words ending with an 's'?

The big deal is that adding possessive apostrophes to words and names like *boss, mews, surplus* and *Thomas*, and to plurals like *cats, hours* and *friends*, is not such a straightforward matter.

Let's look at some examples:

WORDS AND NAMES ENDING WITH 'S'	POSSESSIVE FORM
the boss	the *boss's* temper
Thomas	*Thomas's* recent illness
platypus	*platypus's* eggs
mistress	a *mistress's* secrets
Charles Dickens	*Dickens's* novels

Now see what happens with plural nouns ending with 's':

PLURAL WORDS ENDING WITH 'S'	POSSESSIVE FORM
Penny's parents	Penny's *parents'* house
her friends	her *friends'* parties
the members	the *members'* badges
our employees	our *employees'* bonuses
the girls	the *girls'* classroom

So far, the application of possessive apostrophes seems reasonably systematic and logical, enabling us to distinguish the different meanings. When we read,

> The opera star heard the girl's singing

we understand that only one girl is singing, whereas

> The opera star heard the girls' singing

tells us that the diva is listening to many girls (plural) singing.

From all this we learn that for singular ownership we simply add *'s*, but for plural or shared ownership we add the apostrophe after the *s*.

But there are the usual irritating exceptions. As we've seen, with some plurals, those not ending with 's', the apostrophe comes before the 's' and not after:

> The men's changing room
> The old folk's belongings

Then there are some free choices, where according to taste we can:

ADD THE 'S	*Tom Jones's songs; Glynis's career*
DROP THE FINAL S	*Wales' ruggedness; Dickens' characters; Jesus' teachings*

OBSERVE	*Queens' College Cambridge;*
TRADITION	*Queen's College, Oxford;*
	Queen's University, Belfast; St
	Giles' Cathedral, Edinburgh

Some sticky patches still remain. Watch for adjectives that look like possessives like *games mistress* and which require no apostrophe. Watch also for units of time, like *a day's work, a minute's delay* and *six month's salary* in complex sentences such as these:

> I'm taking three weeks holiday in three weeks' time.
> An hour's delay or two hours' delay – I wish the airline would make up its mind!

So far we've dealt with the problems of possessive nouns and proper nouns. But pronouns can be perplexing, too: some have apostrophes and some do not.

PRONOUNS WITH	*one's problems; anyone's idea;*
APOSTROPHES	*someone's shoes; one another's*
	responsibilities; nobody's fault;
	anybody's luggage; each other's
	possessions

PRONOUNS	*his; hers; its; ours; yours; theirs*
WITHOUT	
APOSTROPHES	

One of the most frequent errors is the use of *it's* for the possessive form of *it*. This is wrong, of course: *it's* is the accepted contraction for *it is* or *it has*.

Contraction Apostrophes

George Bernard Shaw, campaigning for simplified spelling and punctuation, tried to encourage the nation to do without contraction apostrophes – *cant,*

HOUSE OF COMMONS
LONDON SW1A 0AA

Dear Mr Major,

I am writing following you're recalledged remarks on 23rd July that you are the Leader "of a party that is still harking back to a golden age that never was but is now invented."

We in the Labour Party have never believed the Thatcher years to have been a "golden age" but it is not so widely known by the public and you're own party that these views are held by yourself. The country deserves to know exactly were you stand on these matters.

On many occaisions - not least on the day that you became Prime Minister - you applauded what you then claimed to be the achievements of your predecessor. We are entitled to know which are the deluded members of your cabinet and party and what they are deluded about.

Yours sincerely,

H. Harman

Harriet Harman MP
Shadow Chief Secretary to the Treasury

Letter of July 27, 1993 to Prime Minister John Major from Labour's Shadow Chief Secretary to the Treasury, Harriet Harman. Apart from three spelling errors, there are two misuses of *you're* for your.

From the *Sun*, 28.7.93

wont, Ive, arent, etc. – but where he failed, the
Washington Post succeeded spectacularly, though
unwittingly. According to the American author Bill
Bryson, the newspaper once published an article
which confused the possessive *its* with the contraction
it's no less than five times:

> 'Its the worst its been in the last five years . . . Its
> awful . . . Its come full circle . . . Its nice to see
> the enemy.'

I have pointed out that this *its/it's* dilemma is an
alarmingly common one. So here, once and for all:

POSSESSION	The *Washington Post* said its punctuation record was unmatchable by any other newspaper.
CONTRACTION	It's (It is) a fact that the punctuation record of the *Washington Post* isn't (is not) so hot after all.

Also for the record is this list of most of the accepted
contractions:

aren't	*are not*
can't	*cannot; can not*
couldn't	*could not*
hasn't	*has not*
haven't	*have not*
he'll	*he will; he shall*
he's	*he is; he has*
I'd	*I would; I had*
I'm	*I am*
it's	*it is; it has*
I've	*I have*
let's	*let us*
ma'am	*madam*
mustn't	*must not*

she'll	she will; she shall
she's	she is; she has
there's	there is
they'll	they will; they shall
they're	they are
they've	they have
we'll	we will; we shall
weren't	were not
we've	we have
who's	who is
won't	will not
wouldn't	would not
you'll	you will; you shall
you're	you are
you've	you have

Those are conventional, everyday contractions made possible by the apostrophe. But the apostrophe has been used to create many more irregular and creative expressions: 'concertina' combinations like *sweet 'n' low* and *shake 'n' bake*; accent renditions like *'alf a mo'* and *Ah'm talkin' to yuh*; slangy cut-downs like *finger lickin'* and *nuthin' doin'* not to mention the pluralisation of numbers and abbreviations: *1890's*, *MP's*, *CV's* and *IOU's*.

But even as we breathe, such contractions are being further contracted by dropping the apostrophe. This is nothing new, of course: today's *phone* was a *'phone* on its transition from *telephone*; a *bus* was a *'bus* and before that an *omnibus*; and a baby's *pram* was a *p'ram*, out of *peram* from *perambulator*. And so it goes: *1890s*, *MPs*, *CVs*, *IOUs* . . .

A self test follows opposite, but before you attempt it, commit to memory the following:

- *it's* is the abbreviaton for *it is* or *it has*; *its* indicates possession
- *who's* is short for *who is or who has*; *whose* indicates possession

The Retreating Apostrophe

If **Harrod's** advertise their store as **Harrod's**,
why, then, does **Lloyd's Bank** call itself **Lloyds
Bank plc**? What's happened to the possessive
apostrophes in **Missing Persons Bureau,
Pears Soap, Womens Institute** and **Gas
Consumers Council**? **Harrod's** is not only
strict about its name but also strictly correct:
Harrod's is a contraction of *Harrod's store*, or
the store belonging to Harrod. But today there
is a tendency towards simplification (and
perhaps also a recognition of customers' troubles
with apostrophes) and the *'s* is being dropped
wholesale by many businesses and institutions.
Just the same, remember **McDonald's,
Sadler's Wells, Regent's Park, Ladbroke's**
and – to confuse you – **Lloyd's List** and **Lloyd's
Register**.

Apostrophe Self-test

If you've (you have) resisted an attack of apostrophe
apoplexy, try the following test:

1 Which of these versions do you prefer?

   A *The Dean of St Paul's sermon.*
   B *The Dean of St Pauls' sermon.*
   C *The Dean of St Pauls's sermon.*

2 What's the difference between these two statements?

   A *Joan and Eric's parents*
   B *Joan's and Eric's parents*

3 Where would you place the apostrophes in these sentences?

    A   *Cant you see Im busy?*
    B   *Thomass love affair with Jeans sister is off*
    C   *Mines a Budweiser. Whats yours?*

4 Is there anything wrong with this sentence?

King George the Second's and George the Third's reigns saw a great expansion of Britains overseas interests.

5 Can you punctuate this statement?

Will the witnesses please come forward.

Answers, page 112

Punctuation Pot-pourri

We're now sifting through the litter of punctuation but there are still gems to be found: a few dots here, a stroke there, stars, bullets and daggers . . . and all of them can be put to work on occasional odd jobs.

The Three-dot Ellipsis

The science fiction pioneer H. G. Wells is credited with the invention of a mark so ridiculously simple that it is hard to believe it needed inventing at all: the *three-dot ellipsis*. What this line of three dots does is indicate missing matter, thus, more or less saying, 'over to you, reader, work it out for yourself'.

The omitted matter may be a single word, as in this euphemistic statement:

Get the . . . out of here!

Or matter considered to be non-essential:

Yesterday the shares stood at just over £4 which
if you believe last night's closing statement . . .
at that price the company is valued at almost £1.6
billion.

Or an implied quotation or phrase which the reader is
expected to know:

So then she bought contact lenses . . . you
know, men don't make passes . . . she really
believes that, by the way, but anyway she looks
great.

From undertaking the task of signalling omissions the
three dots have acquired other, more subtle
functions:

INDICATING AN UNFINISHED THOUGHT	The problem was, would she sue, or . . .
	Frederick introduced them and, well, you can guess the rest . . .
	He considered the consequences; it would be great to be a hero, but on the other hand . . .
INDICATING TIME LAPSE	Kimball crashed to the pavement with eye-wincing force . . . only later, much later in the darkness, did he realise he'd been the hunted, not the hunter.

INDICATING PAUSE OF DESPAIR	Those long, embittered wails of betrayal, of impassioned pleading, surfacing out of the ex-colonial darkness ... why should anyone bother to listen?
INDICATING DISJOINTED SPEECH	She paced the room. 'I don't know ... every way I look at it ... what would *you* do?' She drew deeply on the cigarette. 'I mean, surely he wouldn't do this to me ... or would he?'

Asterisks and Bullets

A recent letter to *The Sunday Times* complained:

'In your paper last week I noticed a f***, a b****** and a f***ing and this made me wonder just who you think comprises your readership. If you feel that you have to censor any word that could possibly upset anybody, why do we not have M*****l H****tine, the M********t Treaty and the ****** Agricultural ******?'*

Apart from this fairly obvious duty of sanitisation, the asterisk is customarily used to guide the reader to a footnote or explanation elsewhere in the text, thus:

* *Michael Heseltine, Maastricht Treaty, Common Agricultural Policy*

In our busy age the **bullet** has found increasing favour, perhaps because:

- It is the quickest, most direct way to summarise a series of facts or conclusions.
- It energetically signals to the eye that here are the essentials.
- It encourages writers to be brief: using words and phrases rather than sentences.
- It captures readers who are too lazy or too harassed to read solid texts.

The Stroke

Fancily called the virgule, solidus, shilling mark, slash, diagonal and separatrix, the oblique stroke has a few limited uses:

TO INDICATE OPTIONS	*It depends upon how he/she behaves.* *The situation calls for guile and/or force.*
TO SEPARATE LINES OF VERSE	*The mist as it rises/ touched with gold of the morning/ Veils over the sadness/ and the spirit lifts, soaring . . .*
TO ABBREVIATE	*C/- or C/o* = **Care of** *A/c* = **Account** *km/h* = **kilometres per hour**

Italics, Bold and Underlining

In their roles as tools for separating, highlighting and clarifying printed matter, these devices are on the margins of punctuation. Although they can hardly apply to handwritten prose, in this word-processing age the italic, bold and underline keys make possible a useful range of typographic effects. Most of them have been used in this book:

FOR EMPHASIS	Do **not** use a capital letter after a colon.
TO DISTINGUISH A WORD OR WORD GROUP	Less than a century ago, **today** was hyphenated as **to-day**.
TO IDENTIFY A QUOTATION OR AN EXTRACT	The *Oxford English Dictionary* describes a sentence as *Such portion of a composition or utterance as extends from one full stop to another.*
TO INDICATE TITLES	Several errors involving quotation marks will be found in Jane Austen's *Persuasion*.
TO INDICATE A FOREIGN WORD OR PHRASE	The movement's meetings were always heavy with *Sturm und Drang*, shouting and argument and blatant self-importance.

It's worthwhile mentioning that once a foreign word or phrase is generally understood and accepted into the English language (remember that English is a rampant borrower and thief) it need not be italicised or highlighted. Such words include, for example, guru, vis-à-vis, sauerkraut, patisserie, shiatsu and flamenco. If in doubt, consult your dictionary.

Answers to Self-Tests

Semicolon Self-test *(From page 56)*

1 A simple comma is all that's required here:

   Everyone is wary of the cliff, the face of which has weathered alarmingly.

2 The same applies to the second example, in which the first comma can be deleted as unnecessary:

   The couple scarcely knew anyone and were slow to form friendships, having little enthusiasm for new faces.

3 Replace the comma after *acceptable* with a semicolon, or, alternatively, join the two thoughts with a conjunction like *and*:

   It should be stressed that Stephanie's behaviour is unacceptable; it should be brought to her notice immediately.

4 There is potential confusion here. Is the 'groom and watchman' one person doing both jobs, or two different people? Use semicolons to make the sentence clear and easy to follow:

   The Austen household consisted of a cook, laundress, two maids and a butler; a groom; a watchman; and a head gardener and an under-gardener.

5 To construct a sentence like this you need to know your punctuation. There are several places where commas and semicolons would be optional, but I would rewrite it as follows:

Having lost his job in the recession; having had the ill-luck to lose his home and possessions to the bank; having, on top of everything, his wife leave him . . . Patrick was perhaps justified in feeling bitter.

Yes, yes, I know! Many of you would view the three dots as a cop-out, but I would justify their use here on the grounds that anyone reciting this mounting catalogue of disasters would finally become speechless with exasperation, perhaps thinking, 'I mean, how much can the poor guy take!' It is this unvoiced reaction that is represented by the three-dot ellipsis.

Answers to Hyphen Quiz *(From page 89)*

1 (b) **unselfconscious**
2 (a) **10-year-old child**
3 (b) **all-star cast**
4 (b) **50-odd years** – without the hyphen those fifty years would have been very odd indeed!
5 (c) This version is wholly correct. It avoids the 'floater' (part-) and has both *part-time* and *full-time* consistent with hyphens
6 (a) Although it is hardly important, the accepted form is **ups and downs**, unhyphenated.

Apostrophe Self-test *(From page 105)*

1 **B** *St Pauls* is spelt thus, therefore the apostrophe would fall after the 's'.
2 In **A**, Joan and Eric share the same parents, whereas in **B** Joan and Eric have different parents.
3 **A** *Can't you see I'm busy?*
   B *Thomas's love affair with Jean's sister is off.*
   C *Mine's a Budweiser. What's yours?*
4 The sentence is correct except for the missing apostrophe in *Britain's*.
5 It's correct except that it should have a question mark instead of a full stop.